GREGORIAN CHANT

GREGORIAN CHANT

A TEXTBOOK FOR SEMINARIES, NOVITIATES
AND SECONDARY SCHOOLS

by

REV. ANDREW F. KLARMANN

Published by
GREGORIAN INSTITUTE OF AMERICA
TOLEDO, OHIO

Imprimatur
✠ MOST REV. THOMAS E. MOLLOY, S.T.D.
Bishop of Brooklyn

Nihil Obstat
REV. JOHN F. DONOVAN
Censor Librorum

JANUARY 27, 1945

Desclée and Company of Tournai, Belgium, has granted permission to the author to use the rhythmic marks in this textbook.

COPYRIGHT, 1945, BY GREGORIAN INSTITUTE
PRINTED IN U.S.A.   ALL RIGHTS RESERVED

Dedicated to
MOST REVEREND THOMAS E. MOLLOY
BISHOP OF BROOKLYN

FOREWORD

In the following pages Father Klarmann presents a clear, orderly, systematic treatment of liturgical chant.

At the very beginning of his treatise he provides an explanation of certain fundamental terms, such as notation, signs, rhythm, chant structure, etc., which is very serviceable in preparing the reader for the fuller development of the general theme in the subsequent chapters of this book.

With the same thought and purpose the author more particularly gives an early definition of the chief subject of discussion, namely, chant, which he defines, in the usually accepted sense, as liturgical music in the form of plain song, which is monophonic, unaccompanied and free in rhythm. Very interestingly also chant structure is explained. The author then proceeds to record the historical development of chant at least in its salient features.

It is readily understood of course that the Infant Church could not promote a notable advancement in liturgical music during the period of ruthless persecution. And still it seems quite certain that even in the catacombs hymns were used in connection with religious worship. Tertullian and later Eusebius, Augustine and Jerome moreover give testimony regarding the traditional custom of the Church in sponsoring antiphonal and responsorial chant as well as the singing of hymns in relation to sacred service.

After the period of early trial and tribulation the Church was free to foster a definite type of liturgical chant which in content, form and spirit would be appropriate particularly in praising and glorifying God. And the Church, as history convincingly testifies, took full advantage of this opportunity.

A word of special tribute for this progress in the development of chant is due to St. Ambrose who contributed so substantially to the realization of the aim of the Church in this regard by systematizing and establishing within his own Diocese of Milan what is known as the Ambrosian Chant. Later Pope Celestine introduced Ambrosian Chant to Rome.

We know, moreover, that during the fourth century the Papal Choir was established as well as the Schola Lectorum in which boys destined for the Papal Choir were taught the chanting of the lessons of the Mass.

Notwithstanding the prominence and importance which chant thus attained in liturgical service it gradually began to acquire very objectionable features. In his book entitled: *"Church Music—Its Origin and Different Forms,"* Janssens refers to this unsatisfactory change in these words: "People did not relish the chant, and music, substituted to please them, degenerated into worldly, light and frivolous songs which evoked the bulls of popes and the decrees of councils."

To Pope Gregory the Great a fairly reliable and constant tradition, as the author of this book indicates, ascribes the necessary and authoritative standardization of the Roman Chant. Pope Pius XI made impressive reference to this fact when he wrote: "It was in the Lateran Palace that Gregory the Great, having made his famous collection of the traditional treasures of plain song, editing them with additions of his own, wisely founded his great Schola in order to perpetuate a true interpretation of the liturgical chant." (*Divini Cultus sanctitatem.* Dec. 20, 1928.)

Father Klarmann also alludes to the fact that during succeeding centuries the norms, earlier established in this matter, were either forgotten or disregarded and musicians again changed the chant to satisfy popular taste and to provide more entertaining melodies.

The Council of Trent consequently expressed a strong protest against the custom of using secular themes in the composition of sacred music and also against the practice of sacrificing the test for melodic effect.

Later still corrective measures were necessary and in this regard we may note that Father Klarmann gives deserved recognition to the Benedictine monks of Solesmes, who, towards the end of the nineteenth century, started a movement to restore the simplicity, purity and reverence of the chant.

It is perhaps useful to recall that Pope Pius X declared the Solesmes version of the chant to be the official version and it is appropriate also I am sure to point out that schools of liturgical music immediately sprung up in various dioceses to promote systematically the reform in church music thus decreed.

Pope Pius XI stressed the requirements of the Motu Proprio of Pius X and exhorted the clergy and laity to restore approved liturgical music to churches.

Now the question may arise why does the Church establish her own form of music and insist upon its conformity to certain norms? The reason undoubtedly is that the chant is associated with religious functions and more particularly with the Mass, the center of Catholic worship, and therefore the chant must be in conformity with the place, time and purpose of Divine worship. It should be therefore sacred and not profane music.

Then again true religious music is but an exalted prayer—an exultant expression of religious feeling. In making this observation there is suggested at once an appropriate quotation from St. Paul: "Speaking to yourselves in psalms and hymns and spiritual canticles, singing and making melody in your hearts to the Lord." (Eph. V: 19.)

And in further reference to the prayerful function of liturgical chant Sister Mary Gael, of Marygrove College, very pertinently and piously observes: "It is not difficult to understand how the simple flow of pure melody carrying words of the sacred text can speak to the soul of God and then lead the soul to speak to God in prayer."

Sometimes perhaps the impression might be developed that the church chant represents a type of inferior music at least in comparison with secular musical compositions.

In dealing with such an unfortunate and incorrect impression it might be well to quote Professor Willi Apel, of Harvard University, who, in his *Dictionary of Music*, published in 1944, remarks: "Whereas formerly musicians looked disdainfully on Gregorian chant, particularly because it 'lacks' harmony, it is now becoming more and more fully recognized as an unsurpassed treasure of purely melodic music. In particular, its freely flowing rhythm, far from being chaotic, shows subtleties of structure and organization which are doubtless superior to the comparatively platitudinous devices of rhythm in harmonized music, with its meter, measures, beats, regular phrases, etc."

Then again competent musicians have admitted the superior quality and in fact the supreme excellence of church chant. I refer to such capable critics as Witt. Gevaert, Halevy, Mozart, Berlioz. (*Catholic Encyclopedia.*) Halevy, for instance, observes: "The chant is the most beautiful religious melody that exists on earth." Then there is Mozart's statement, that he would gladly exchange all his music for the fame of having composed the Gregorian Preface.

In view therefore of its use in religious worship; of its formal approval by the Church and of its inherent simplicity, purity and excellence we may readily agree that Father Klarmann has rendered a highly meritorious service in trying to promote a truer understanding, deeper appreciation and more extensive use of Gregorian Chant.

THOMAS E. MOLLOY,
Bishop of Brooklyn

Brooklyn, New York
June 25, 1945

INTRODUCTION

If we were to adopt the medieval style of designating this book, we might entitle it "A Practical Commentary on all the Features of Gregorian Chant, with Special Attention Given to the Principles of Rhythm as Proposed and Formulated by the Monks of Solesmes." Using this modern method of introduction, however, we state that this is a textbook containing all the features of the chant, explained in such a way that a person with little or no musical training could acquire sufficient knowledge of the subject to be able to sing the chant with correctness, propriety and beauty. This book is intended, therefore, for those in seminaries, novitiates, secondary schools and other institutions of learning whose curriculum includes a study of the chant, as well as for choirmasters, their singers and for all others who may be interested in this branch of musical art.

A cursory examination of the Table of Contents or of the book itself will reveal that it is divided into three parts. The first three chapters of Part I are a technical explanation of the signs and figures of the chant as they appear in print, and of the means by which long notes are designated. The following nine chapters deal with the theory of rhythm, its analysis, its purpose and the method by which this purpose is achieved. Illustrations are taken, for the most part, from the Requiem Mass and the Ordinary. Chapters IV to XII follow in logical order and it is suggested that they be studied or read to best advantage in the sequence in which they appear. The remaining two chapters of Part I present incidental, but none the less important, reflections on the chant. Part II includes a treatment of the more difficult or more advanced aspects of chant (modes, psalmody), of Latin pronunciation, indispensable in the proper singing of the chant. Part III includes treatises on the relation between the Mass and the chant, the history of church music, and finally the rules of the Church regarding music during a liturgical function.

Throughout the textbook we have tried as far as possible to avoid the use of technical language. For example, the term "fall group" is used instead of "thesis" and "rise group" instead of "arsis." Even in treating the nature of a Latin word the term "rise" is sometimes adopted for the accented syllable and "fall" for the grave syllable of a word. The translations of the Greek and Latin names for the neumes are supplied as a teaching aid since the picture conjured up by the English word is more graphic than the foreign term, especially in the teaching of younger students.

The author wishes to express his gratitude to the monks of Solesmes, particularly to Dom Gajard, who commended upon the ideas of rhythm contained in this textbook which was written in substance during the author's stay at the monastery; to Right Reverend Monsignor Lawrence Bracken, Chairman of the Diocesan Commission for Church Music in the Diocese of Brooklyn, for his encouragement and valuable advice; and, lastly, to Doctor Clifford Bennett, without whose cooperation this book would never have been as practical as it may be and without whose interest it might never have been published.

A. F. K.

TABLE OF CONTENTS

Foreword... iii
Introduction.. vii

Part I

Chapter		Page
I.	Gregorian Notation and Signs....................	1
II.	Neumes or Combinations of Notes................	11
III.	The Duration of Notes..........................	18
IV.	The Nature of Rhythm..........................	23
V.	The Development of Rhythm....................	27
VI.	The Purpose of Rhythm.........................	34
VII.	The Uniting of Notes in Neumatic Chants.........	36
VIII.	The Uniting of Notes in Syllabic Chants...........	42
IX.	The Uniting of Groups of Notes..................	54
X.	The Uniting of Groups into Divisions and of Divisions into Phrases...................................	58
XI.	The Joining of Divisions........................	65
XII.	The Application of the Principles of Rhythm to Special Figures...................................	67
XIII.	Directing the Chant............................	75
XIV.	The Application of Gregorian Principles to Modern Music...	77

Part II

XV.	Gregorian Modes...............................	82
XVI.	Psalmody......................................	90
XVII.	Latin Pronunciation............................	104

Part III

XVIII.	The Mass and the Chant........................	113
XIX.	The History of Church Music....................	121
XX.	Church Music Legislation.......................	131

General Index....................................... 144

ix

PART I

CHAPTER I

GREGORIAN NOTATION AND SIGNS

1. Gregorian melodies are written on a staff of four lines and three spaces, while modern music is written on a staff of five lines and four spaces. The notes are for the most part square in shape, preserving their original character of a dot or period made with a quill. Notes are found also in other forms for different purposes and effects, as will be explained in subsequent chapters.

2. The notes indicated on the lines or in the spaces of the staff represent those of the sol-fa system. These notes are conventionally called: *do, re, mi, fa, sol, la* and *ti*. We shall often have occasion to replace them by numbers in such a way that 1 will represent *do;* 2, *re;* 3, *mi;* etc. Notes above the middle octave will be distinguished by a dot over them: 6 7 1̇ 2̇; those below this octave, by a dot under them: 6̣ 7̣ 1 2.

3. The sol-fa scale consists of eight notes comprising an octave. Each of the eight notes is one whole tone from the preceding, except *fa* and *do* which are only a half tone higher than *mi* and *ti* respectively. The following scheme shows the scale steps and the number designation to be used throughout this book:

$$\overset{\frac{1}{2}\text{ tone}}{\frown} \qquad \overset{\frac{1}{2}\text{ tone}}{\frown}$$

do	re	mi	fa	sol	la	ti	do
1	2	3	4	5	6	7	1̇

4. The notes of the sol-fa scale are relative in pitch; that is, they are gauged according to the pitch chosen for the key-note or the tonic. They do not represent definite notes on the piano as do the notes on the modern staff. This means that the note *re*, for example, does not refer to a definite note on the piano, but may be any note depending upon the note chosen for *do*. Hence, if the piano note F were chosen for *do*, then G would be *re*, A would be *mi* and B♭ would be *fa*, etc. If, however, E were chosen for *do*, then F♯ would be *re;* G♯ would be *mi*, and A would be *fa*. The reason for the use of sharps lies in the fact that the notes E and F on the piano are only a half tone apart, whereas in the sol-fa scale *do* and *re* are a whole tone apart. In order, therefore, to play the whole tones *do* and *re* when E is chosen for *do*, F♯ must be used for *re*. From this we may readily deduce that any modern key may be used to play

a Gregorian melody provided the intervals on the piano are made to correspond exactly to the intervals of the sol-fa scale. The key in modern music is determined according to the note chosen for *do*. In speaking of the key of F, we simply mean that the F is *do* in that key. For a more detailed exposition of the scales and tonalities of the chant and appropriate keys for the melodies, see Chapter XV.

5. The chant notation uses one of two clefs to designate either *do* or *fa* on the staff. From these notes the other notes may easily be deduced. The two clefs are known as the *do clef*, indicating the position of *do*, and the *fa clef*, indicating the position of *fa*:

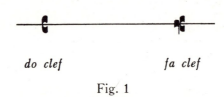

do clef   fa clef

Fig. 1

6. The *do clef* may appear on the second, third or fourth line (from the bottom), but is most frequently found on the third or fourth line; the *fa clef* may appear on the third or fourth line, but it is most frequently found on the third. Neither clef ever appears in any space or on the first line from the bottom. The following staffs will show the various positions of the clefs and their influence on the notes:

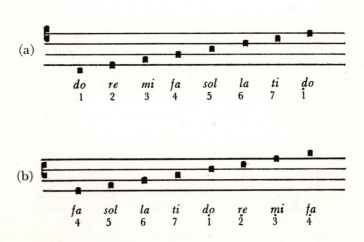

Fig. 2

NOTATION AND SIGNS

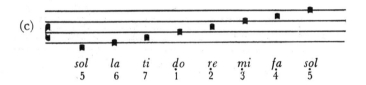

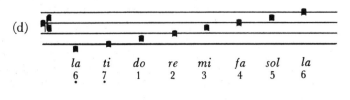

Fig. 2 (cont.)

7. The choice and position of the clef are determined by the range of the melody. That particular clef is chosen and is so located that the melody will fit conveniently within the lines of the staff. When a melody exceeds the limits of the staff, leger lines are used as in modern music.

8. There are no sharps in the chant and only one note may be flatted. That note is *ti*; when flatted it is called *te*. When *te* is represented in number, the 7 is crossed (7̸) to distinguish it from *ti*.

9. *Te* forms a half tone between 6 and 7̸ and a whole tone between 7̸ and 1. The succession of 6 7̸ 1 has the same relation as 3̂4 5, whereas the succession 5 6 7̸ corresponds to 2 3̂4. Since *ti* is the only note that can be altered, composers often resorted to transposition when they wanted a whole tone between 3 and 4. The transposition could be effected either by changing the position of the *do* clef, or by using the *do* clef instead of the *fa* clef. In the following illustration at (a), the desired whole tone between 3 4 is effected by a change of the position of the *do* clef and the flatting of *ti*. At (b), however, the *do* clef is used instead of the *fa* clef, and the *ti* is flatted.

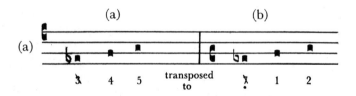

Fig. 3

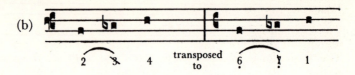

Fig. 3 (cont.)

Very often, however, the use of the flat throughout the entire melody is indicative of a transposed melody (see par. 178).

10. The change of *ti* to *te* is indicated on the staff by the flat sign (♭) and effects only the *ti* over that word on which it occurs. *Te* automatically becomes natural if the flat is not repeated over the next word. (See Fig.4 [a]). If the word extends over a divisional sign (par. 12) the flat likewise loses its force beyond that sign unless it is repeated (b):

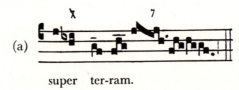

Fig. 4

If *te* is to be naturalized before the end of the word or before the divisional sign, the common natural sign (♮) is used as indication. *Ti* remains natural, then, until the flat sign is definitely repeated.

11. The notes are commonly square in shape, having originated in all probability as dots made with a quill. There are, however, different shapes of notes to indicate different purposes and effects:

    (a) the square punctum ■   (d) the quilisma

    (b) the inclined punctum ♦   (e) the liquescent

    (c) the virga or stem   (f) the guide

Fig. 5

NOTATION AND SIGNS ¶ 11

(a) The **square note** is the ordinary and most common of all the notes. It is used either alone as a punctum or in some combinations (neumes) as will be shown in the next chapter.

(b) The **inclined note** is used only in descending passages in combinations. It does not differ in time value from the square note. The reason for its inclined shape lies in the fact that the ancient scribes slanted the quill when writing such descending notes.

(c) The **virga** or stemmed note is a note with a vertical line at its right or left. This note has no greater time value than the square note. The stem indicates a comparatively high note and is a remnant of the accent sign (/) employed today to indicate the acute accent of a word. Formerly every syllable of the word was marked with either the so-called 'acute' (/) or 'grave' (\) accent:

mì-sé-rì-cór-dì-à

Fig. 6

Later, however, when the grave accent was replaced by a dot made with a quill, the acute accent was replaced by the stemmed note which is the present virga:

◀
mi-se-ri-cor-di-a

Fig. 7

Hence the virga is nothing more than a relatively high note, even as the accented syllables are the high syllables of the word.

(d) The **quilisma** and

(e) The **liquescent** are never found as single notes apart from the combination of notes; their purpose is explained in the next chapter (pars. 35, 43).

(f) The **guide** or **custos,** is a small note of great assistance to the singer. Its various functions as a guide note are illustrated in the following example. At (a) it indicates the first note of the next line; at (b) it indicates the pitch of the next note following a division mark where the clef has been changed.

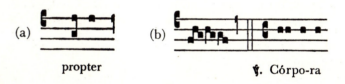

(a) propter   (b) ℣. Córpo-ra

Fig. 8

12. The melodies of the chant are divided and subdivided into musical sections similar to the clauses and phrases that make up a sentence. These divisions are determined by the nature of the melody and text. The marks indicating them may rightly be called 'musical punctuation marks.' Each division is an entity in itself although it may be part of a larger unit, just as a phrase or clause forms part of a sentence. These divisions of the chant are designated by vertical lines cutting one or more lines of the staff:

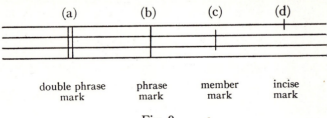

| (a) | (b) | (c) | (d) |
| double phrase mark | phrase mark | member mark | incise mark |

Fig. 9

(a) The **double phrase mark** is a double line cutting all the lines of the staff; it represents the largest and most important division of a melody. It marks the end of a melody and the total completion of the text. When it occurs within a melody, however, (as between the sections of a *Kyrie* or a *Gloria* or *Credo*) it denotes the place where the choirs are to alternate. In the Gradual chants it marks the place where the solo singer is to take up the melody, a place also designated in the text by the **versicle mark** (See Fig. 8 [b]).

(b) The **phrase mark** is a single vertical line cutting all the lines of the staff. It represents the melodic and often textual completion of a section or division. It may be compared with a period in grammar in that it marks the end of a musical sentence and implies a completion that requires a definite pause. It demands a definite softness and slowness on at least the two last groups, and a complete silence of two beats before the next phrase is sung.

(c) The **member** is so called because it is a member or part of a phrase. It implies no completion of melody or text but functions as a convenient punctuation of the phrase. It calls for a slight retard but implies no interruption. If breath must be renewed at this place, it should be 'stolen', as it were, from the previous beat in order to avoid a break in the singing.

(d) The **incise** is the smallest musical subdivision. It subdivides the member just as the member subdivides the phrase. Since the subdivision is subordinate it needs only the slightest retard and definitely no interruption. It may be compared to the comma in writing.

13. Occasionally a comma appears on the fourth line of the staff. Practically speaking, it differs little from the foregoing incise mark and is subject to personal interpretation.

NOTATION AND SIGNS ¶ 14-15

14. In general, melodies are not divided into equal parts as though one incise or member were always as long as the other. The divisions are almost never equal or regular throughout—the Requiem Offertory is a good example of irregular division. The first phrase is made up of three members, each of which embraces two incises; yet the second phrase is formed of three members which are undivided; the third phrase is composed of two members, the second of which is subdivided into two incises, and so forth. The following diagram illustrates these subdivisions:

Requiem Offertory
- 1st phrase
  - 1st member
    - 1st incise: *Domine Jesu Christi*,
    - 2nd incise: *Rex gloriae*,
  - 2nd member
    - 1st incise: *libera animas*
    - 2nd incise: *omnium fidelium defunctorum*
  - 3rd member
    - 1st incise: *de poenis inferni*,
    - 2nd incise: *et de profundo lacu*:
- 2nd phrase
  - 1st member: *libera eas de ore leonis*,
  - 2nd member: *ne absorbeat eas tartarus*,
  - 3rd member: *ne cadant in obscurum*:
- 3rd phrase
  - 1st member: *sed signifer sanctus Michael*
  - 2nd member
    - 1st incise: *repraesentet eas*
    - 2nd incise: *in lucem sanctam*.

In the hymn *Adoro Te*, however, we have an example of symmetrical division. Each stanza is made up of two phrases, composed of two members, each of which is composed of two incises. Each division is equal in length to its corresponding member. Each stanza is divided as follows:

stanza
- 1st phrase
  - 1st member
    - 1st incise: *Adoro Te, devote*,
    - 2nd incise: *latens Deitas*,
  - 2nd member
    - 3rd incise: *Quae sub his figuris*
    - 4th incise: *vere latitas*:
- 2nd phrase
  - 3rd member
    - 5th incise: *Tibi se cor meum*
    - 6th incise: *totum subjicit*,
  - 4th member
    - 7th incise: *quia Te contemplans*
    - 8th incise: *totum deficit*.

15. The **ictus** in print is a short vertical line over or under a note:

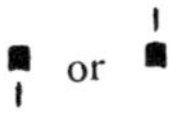

Fig. 10

Its rhythmical significance is explained in Chapter V (see par. 72). Let us say, for the present, that the note on which this sign appears is the rhythmic bearer of the chant. In theory, it is the first note of a group; in practice, it represents a fall note of the rhythm. Not all the fall notes are marked since the majority are self-evident from the rules laid down in succeeding chapters (VII and VIII). Those, however, that carry the sign are so designated to clarify any doubt, to simplify the reading, or to effect a definite rhythmic nuance. It is included here merely as one of the signs used in chant books.

16. The **episema** is a horizontal line over or under one or more notes and indicates that the note or notes are to be prolonged beyond their usual length (see par. 145).

Fig. 11

17. The **asterisk** (*) suggests several directions:

(a) It indicates the end of the intonation when it appears at the beginning of a selection. In the following illustration, the chanter intones the melody up to the asterisk, at which point the choir enters:

Fig. 12

(b) When it occurs toward the end of a selection, it denotes the place where the choir is to re-enter:

di- ne * pér-fru- i.

Fig. 13

(c) When it appears alone, dividing the last *Kyrie* into two parts, it indicates that the section of the choir whose turn it is to sing that particular *Kyrie*, sings the whole of it, and that the other section is to enter at the asterisk:

Fig. 14

But if the *Kyrie* is divided into three parts by a single and a double asterisk, the first section of the choir sings to the first asterisk, the other section sings to the second (from the single to the double asterisk) and all sing from the double asterisk to the end:

Ky- ri- e   *   **   e- lé- i-son.

Fig. 15

(d) When the asterisk occurs in the middle of a psalm verse, it does not call for a change of choir, but indicates the place for the mediant cadence (see par. 198.).

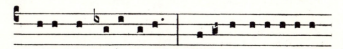

vo-tum in Je-rú- sa-lem: * exáudi o-ra-ti- ó-nem

Fig. 16

18. The letters *ij* or *iij*, found after the *Kyrie's*, *Christe's* or the *Alleluia's*, are signs of repetition. The *ij* indicates that what precedes is to be sung twice while the *iij* calls for a three-fold repetition. The letters are probably an abbreviation of the Latin word *idem* meaning 'the same.' Hence *Kyrie eleison. iij.* indicates that *Kyrie eleison* should be sung three times.

19. Chant melodies are classified according to the richness of melody on the syllables of the text:

(a) **Syllabic chants** are those in which, for the most part, there is one note to the syllable (The Psalms, *Credo* chants, sequences, some hymns, for example, the *Adoro Te*, the Preface and the *Pater Noster* are syllabic in character).

(b) **Neumatic chants** are those in which most of the syllables are adorned with neumes or combinations of notes (some *Gloria* chants, antiphons, and hymns such as the *Verbum supernum*, are neumatic in character).

(c) **Melismatic chants** are those in which most syllables are adorned with many neumes. This is the richest kind of chant (the Graduals, Tracts, and *Alleluia* verses are examples of melismatic chant).

20. Every Gregorian melody, in fact every piece of vocal music, is composed of three elements: melody, rhythm and text. Each of these elements has its place and is governed by separate laws; the

rights of each are for the most part observed. Circumstances arise, nevertheless, which necessitate the precedence of one over the other two. For example, the natural treatment of a word may demand that the last syllable be lower in pitch than the accented syllable. Sometimes, however, the melody and word are so constituted that the last syllable will occur on a high melodic note. In this case the melody asserts its right over and above the word or text. So, also, can rhythm assert its right over the melody or text. A rhythmic rise should be higher in melody than its rhythmic fall. But we often find that the note on which the rhythmic rise occurs is lower in melody than its rhythmic fall. Then again, the last syllable of a word should be set to a rhythmic fall note since the last syllable is the end of the word and the fall note, the end of the rhythm. But still, the rhythm need not respect the word in all cases; it may, therefore, set a rhythmic rise on the last syllable of a word. It is our duty to heed the natural demands of each in so far as it is possible to do so. The recognition of such demands will be taught in later lessons.

21. The melody is designated by the notes on the staff and indicates (1) the pitch of the notes and (2) the number of notes to be sung on each syllable. The pitch is indicated by the position of the notes on the staff. The notes are so printed over each syllable that there is no difficulty in determining the number and kind to be sung on the syllable.

22. The reading of the text should present no difficulty. The language used is Latin, though Greek and Hebrew words also occur. The words *Kyrie eleison* and those heard on Good Friday (*Agios o Theos*, etc.) are Greek. Words like *Hosanna, Alleluia* and *Amen* are Hebrew in origin. Whatever their origin, however, all words are pronounced or sung according to the value of their letters in Latin. This is fully treated in Chapter XVII. The melody will, in the majority of cases, follow the natural rhythmic curve of the word, rising to the accent and falling to rest from it. But, as has been said, it will at times disregard the natural rights of the word and follow its own course.

23. The rhythm is the principle by which the melody and words are given flowing motion. This motion is described by the figure or neume in which the notes are represented, by the occasional ictus mark (par. 15), by the various signs of length (par. 48) and by the divisional marks (par. 12). But these do not adequately indicate clearly all the important features of rhythm. Rhythm is perhaps the most important aspect of the chant, and undeniably it is a salient feature of any musical composition. Yet it is most difficult to consign to print. Furthermore, it is difficult to establish rigid laws for proper rhythmic interpretation, for it is the primary duty of rhythm to respect as far as possible the natural demands of melody and of text. In rendering the chant, therefore, we must be guided by the rule that rhythm, melody and text must be set in as close agreement as is possible. This principle is so important that the major part of this book is devoted to its explanation.

CHAPTER II

NEUMES OR COMBINATIONS OF NOTES

24. Whenever two or more notes are to be sung on one syllable, the notes are arranged above them in figures called *neumes*. The word neume is derived from the Greek, either from *pneuma* meaning 'breath,' or from *neuma* meaning 'sign.' These figures or neumes illustrate the rhythm graphically so that after a little practice the rhythm can easily be read from the scheme in which the notes are arranged. In this respect the ancient Gregorian notation is far superior to our modern notation which has no neumatic figures. Amateurs of the chant should not be discouraged by the strange appearance of notes and neumes. A little effort expended in becoming acquainted with the ancient system will soon be rewarded with facility in reading the rhythm from the figures.

25. Too much stress should not be laid upon the memorization of the Latin or Greek names of these figures. After all, the ability to sing them correctly is our aim. For those who prefer more simple terms the English derivatives of the original foreign-language names have been added. The use of the English terms is especially recommended for younger students of the chant, for it seems unreasonable to burden them with the task of learning foreign names that are unintelligible to them. The foreign names are retained, however, in order to satisfy the more facetious critics.

26. A knowledge of the physical structure of the neumes is necessary for the complete understanding of Gregorian rhythm. A knowledge of the neumes is interrelated with a full knowledge of rhythm: it is difficult to explain one without the knowledge of the other.

27. The neumes probably had their origin in the two grammatical accent signs: the grave accent (\) and the acute (/). Both were made from left to right; the former described by a downward movement; the latter an upward movement. The acute accent was used for a higher note; the grave for a lower note. The combination, therefore, of a high note followed by a lower note was represented in the ancient manuscripts by the circumflex (∧); whereas a low note followed by a higher was represented by its inverse (∨). When several notes descended from the higher or first note, the figure took the shape of /∴ etc. Such, then, is the probable origin of the forerunners of our present neumatic system.

28. Neumes may be divided into three classes: (a) simple; (b) compound; (c) special. A *simple neume* is made up of either two or three notes; a *compound neume* is a simple neume that has been enlarged either by the addition of more notes, or by the combining of two or more neumes; a *special neume* is a simple neume that serves a special purpose.

29. There are three *simple two-note neumes:* the *podatus*, in which the lower note is sung first; the *clivis*, in which the higher note is sung first; and the *bivirga* or *distropha*, in which the two notes are in unison. These simple neumes are illustrated below.

30. The *podatus* or *pes* (from the Greek and Latin words for 'foot'): a neume of two notes, of which the lower is sung first.

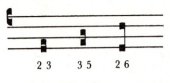

2 3   3 5   2 6

Fig. 17

31. The *clivis* (from the Latin for 'incline'): a neume of two notes, of which the higher is sung first. This higher note always has a virga (par. 11 [c]), a trace of the original acute accent (see par. 11 and 27).

i 7   i 6   i 4

Fig. 18

32. The *bivirga* or *distropha* (Latin and Greek for 'double stem' and 'double comma' respectively): the two notes of this neume are in unison or on the same pitch. The difference between the two forms lies in the fact that the bivirga is used when the two notes form an important rhythmic climax (see par. 124).

4 4   4 4

Fig. 19

33. There are five kinds of *simple three-note neumes*: (1) in which all three ascend; (2) in which all three descend; (3) in which the middle note is highest; (4) in which the middle note is lowest; (5) in

which all three are in unison. The first of these (three notes ascending) subdivides into three classes: (a) in which all the notes are of equal length; (b) in which the first note is prolonged; (c) in which the second note is prolonged. Illustrations and further commentary on these forms are given below.

34. The *scandicus* (from the Latin word for 'ascend'): the three notes ascend and are of equal length or duration. This neume seldom carries any rhythmic sign.

4 5 6   2 4 5

Fig. 20

35. The *quilisma* (from the Greek word for 'turn'): this neume also consists of three notes that ascend, the first of which, however, is prolonged. The quilisma is distinguished from the scandicus in that the middle note is 'wavy.' It is probable that this note was formerly trilled; possibly it is parent to our modern trill or turn sign. One fact concerning the quilisma, however, is certain: the note preceding the wavy one is always to be prolonged. The second and third notes of this neume are rendered smoothly and, compared with the first, rather briefly.

6 7 1̇

Fig. 21

The quilisma exerts a retroactive influence on the notes approaching it in such a way that the closer they are to it, the longer are they held. The note immediately before the quilisma, however, is never as long as two beats. In this way the following beautiful melodic figure of the Requiem Introit is given due prominence and grandeur. As the notes before the quilisma approach it, they grow longer in deference to it.

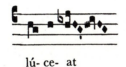

lú- ce- at

Fig. 22

36. The *salicus* (from the Latin for 'leap'): in this neume the second note is always prolonged. We may readily see the reason for its name, for the first note represents the brief 'leap' upon the syllable; the second note, being long, represents a slight settling upon the syllable; and the third, the brief leap from the syllable. This neume is distinguished from the scandicus in that it always bears the rhythmic ictus over or under its second note.

4 5 6 6 7 3̇ 4 1̇ 2̇

Fig. 23

37. The *climacus* (from the Latin for 'ladder'): in this neume all three notes descend. The first always has the virga; the others are inclined notes (See par. 11 [b]).

6 5 4 6 4 3

Fig. 24

38. The *torculus* (from the Latin word pertaining to 'a press' — a meaning exemplified by the shape of the neume). In this neume the middle note is highest and is to be sung smoothly.

2 3 2 2 4 2 1 4 3

Fig. 25

39. The *porrectus* (from the Latin for 'extension'): this neume consists of three notes, the middle of which is lowest. It is the reverse of the torculus although its construction differs from it. The first note is at the left of the curved bar; the second is at the right of the curved bar; and the third is obviously a square note. It should be noted that the first and second notes of this neume are incorporated within the sweeping black stroke of the neume.

6 5 6 1̇ 6 7

Fig. 26

NEUMES

40. The *tristopha* (from the Greek for 'triple comma'): a neume of three notes, all of them in unison. In order to keep the choir together on these notes, and to add a delightful nuance, each note is to be sung with a very slight percussive attack.

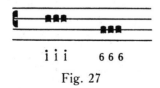

i i i   6 6 6

Fig. 27

41. In former editions of the chant, the so-called *'oriscus'* consisted of a slightly inverted square note affixed to the last note of a neume, more frequently, to the last note of a torculus. In more modern editions its place is taken by an ordinary square note. According to Dom Mocquereau (Le Nombre Musical Gregorien II, pg. 377, par. 499) it changes neither the rhythm nor the melody of the neume to which it is added. It does, however, have a retroactive effect, that is, it informs the chanter that the foregoing neume is to be rendered with utmost delicacy and smoothness. Since it is no longer printed as an oriscus and since it effects neither the rhythm nor the melody, it is excluded from the present classification of the neumes.

    in ancient editions   in modern editions

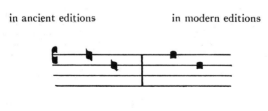

Fig. 28

42. The *compound neumes* are either enlargements or combinations of simple neumes. They can be easily recognized if the simple neumes are known. There is, however, a peculiarity in the formation of the neume compounded with the torculus. When a note is added to the torculus the figure looks as if it were a porrectus with a note before it.

Fig. 29

And so, too, when two notes are added to it:

Fig. 30

43. Under *special neumes* are enumerated the so-called *'liquiscents'* (meaning 'smooth-flowing'). They are distinguished from ordinary neumes in that the last note is printed smaller than the preceding note or notes. They do not differ from the ordinary neume in melody or rhythm. Their sole purpose is to facilitate and beautify the singing. In chanting we pass from the vowel sound of one syllable to the vowel sound of the next, briskly but clearly inserting the consonants that occur between them. Thus, for example, in singing *Do - mi - nus*, the vowel sound of the syllables *o*, *i*, and *u* are sustained but the consonants *d*, *m*, *n* and *s* are quickly sounded in their place before or after the vowel. But between the principle vowels of the syllables there may be and often are other vowels. For example, the three principle vowels in the word *exaudi*, from the Requiem Introit, are *e*, *a* and *i*. The *sol* over the second syllable is sung on the *-a*; *la* is printed as a liquescent on which *-u-* is sung.

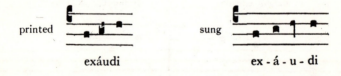

Fig. 31

Among the consonants that appear between the vowel sounds, there are some that are singable and sustainable. These are called 'semi-vowels' because they are so much like vowels in their production. A vowel is a sound that allows the air to pass freely through the mouth without the interference of the tongue, teeth or lips. A semi-vowel also allows the air to pass freely but because there is a slight interference of the tongue, lips or teeth, or any combination of them, they can be sung to a definite note and sustained. The semi-vowels are *l*, *m*, *n*, *r* and *ng*. When these semi-vowels appear at the end of a syllable, that syllable is sustained on the principle vowel and the semi-vowel is sung to the liquescent note, as was illustrated in the case of the vowel *u* in the word *exaudi*. In other words, the semi-vowel is rendered as though it formed a diphthong with the principle vowel. The soft, pleasant variety of the delicate shade of the semi-vowels in contrast to the lengthier tone of the actual vowel

NEUMES ¶ 43

sounds adds a beautiful nuance to the singing (see par. 253). The following illustration gives the ordinary and the liquescent form of the various neumes:

Fig. 32

The following illustration shows the proper method of singing the words *lauda*, *Sanctus* and *Alleluia*, which are generally written with liquescent neumes. The singer must bear in mind, however, that the whole of the extra vowel or semi-vowel is not sung to the liquescent, for this note is merely a help for its proper rendition.

Fig. 33

CHAPTER III

THE DURATION OF NOTES

44. The contrast between long and short notes in the chant is so important, as we shall see in succeeding chapters, that a special chapter will be devoted to an explanation of their difference and appearance in print and to the methods by which the long notes are indicated.

45. In paragraph 20 we dealt with the interrelation of melody, rhythm and text. A note, as we see it in Gregorian notation, has a definite rhythmic character, a definite pitch, and is to be sung to a definite syllable of the text. Every note in the chant is, therefore, influenced by these three features. As a rhythmic entity it is either a rise note or a fall note; as a melodic entity it is either high or low. Furthermore, it is sung to a syllable of a word which is either a grave or an acute accented syllable. For this reason it is quite incorrect to say that all notes are exactly equal in time value even though they may appear to be equal in print. Every rhythmic rise note is slightly briefer than a rhythmic fall note precisely because of its rhythmic character; and, on the other hand, the note on the accented syllable of the word will always be slightly briefer than that on the last syllable because the accented syllable is briefer in speech than the other. In this way the features of melody, rhythm and text will influence the length of a note.

46. How is one to determine the time value of an ordinary note in Gregorian notation? By an ordinary note we mean one which is *not to be prolonged*. When Gregorian melodies are transcribed into modern notation, the ordinary note is represented by the modern eighth note (♪). A long note may be represented by a quarter note (♩), or by an extended eighth (♪). This, however, indicates only the relative value. What is the length of the ordinary note in Gregorian Chant? Each ordinary note has the time value of a syllable spoken in ordinary discourse. This is what the square note originally intended to convey. (See par. 11 [c]). To find the tempo of a piece of Gregorian music we need only recite the words of the text in a devout fashion; the time value given to each syllable will be the time value of the ordinary note. The chant should never be either dragged or rushed. It must be remembered that every Gregorian selection is a prayer — whether of adoration, praise, supplication or petition. No one should attempt to sing the chant without the firm realization that the song is a prayer, a prayer which must

DURATION OF NOTES

spring from a lively faith and profound love toward Him whom we address in song. The living faith will then rid the chant of all sluggishness, but the profound love will check all speed.

47. The secret of the simple beauty of the chant is hidden within the steady and uninterrupted pulsation of each note. The time value of the ordinary note is called the 'basic pulsation'. The basic pulsation must be maintained evenly throughout the piece. This observation may, at first hand, appear superfluous, but it has been noted that more errors in singing are committed on this point than on any other. Whether the notes are high or low in pitch, their basic pulsation must be maintained constantly. Frequently in the more elaborate chants we may find as many as thirty or forty notes on one syllable, as for instance in the following excerpt from the Requiem Gradual, yet, in the same piece some syllables are given but one note:

ae-tér-   na

Fig. 34

Nevertheless, whether there are many notes or only one note to the syllable, the basic pulsation of each ordinary note is the same. There must be no slackening of speed on the syllables with single notes, nor acceleration on those of many notes, for the basic pulsation is even throughout the selection.

48. Every note, then, is of equal duration except those that are marked long. The following signs of length are used: (1) the dot; (2) the episema (par. 16); (3) repetition; (4) the pressus; (5) specific notes in some neumes.

49. The **dotted note:** a dot added to a note doubles its value; that is, it prolongs its time value to two beats. Within a division a dotted note has the value of two ordinary beats. At the cadence, however, where greater length is indicated, the dotted note will be prolonged to two slow beats.

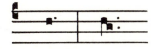

Fig. 35

The word 'cadence' is derived from the Latin word *cadere* meaning 'to fall'. By a cadence, therefore, we mean a fall in rhythm, as that which occurs at the end of the divisions (see par. 12.) As the division is of greater or less importance, the cadence will accordingly demand a greater or less retard or slackening of tempo; the incise will be accorded a very slight cadence or retard, the member with a more pronounced retard, but the phrase with a very definite slackening of tempo. This will be explained more fully in a subsequent chapter.

50. The **episema** (par. 16): a horizontal line over or under one or more notes. This mark does not necessarily prolong the note to two beats but merely indicates that the note or notes should be extended beyond their ordinary value. (For further discussion see par. 145.)

Fig. 36

The episema over or under the note of a podatus, however, is a special case (see 3rd and 4th neume in Fig. 36). An episema under the neume indicates that only the first or lower note is to be prolonged; the sign over the neume tells that both notes are to be prolonged beyond their natural value.

51. **Repetition:** a note may be prolonged by the addition of other notes in unison to it. The addition may be made to a single note, as in the following example from the Requiem Gradual:

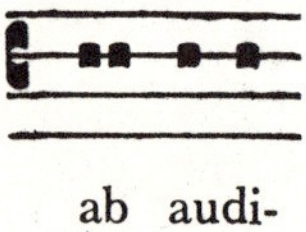

ab audi-

Fig. 37

or to the first or last note of a neume, as the sign over *Re-* in *Requiem*, from the Requiem Introit, and the sign over *-ne* of *Domine* from the Gradual:

Ré-qui- em   mi- ne:

Fig. 38

This kind of prolongation is used in active passages while the dotted note is used in rather restful passages of the rhythm.

DURATION OF NOTES ¶ 52

52. The **pressus:** in order to procure certain rhythmic effects two neumes are often so fused that the last note of one and the first note of the next form one long note. As examples we may refer to the pressus (clivis and porrectus) over *-ter-* from the Requiem Introit:

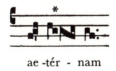

ae -tér - nam

Fig. 39

over *-la* (podatus and clivis; two clives), and over the *ju-* (climacus and clivis) of the Gradual:

- la   ju-   stus:

Fig. 40

In the Tract of the Requiem Mass there are three pressi over *-ctorum* of *defunctorum* and four over the *-i* of *perfrui*:

de- functó - rum

pér-fru- i.

Fig. 41

Some authors do not distinguish between a repetition and a pressus. Such a distinction should be made because of the different rhythmic effect. A pressus always implies a slight 'pressure' or stress on its first note; that is, on the first note of length. The stress is light if the figure occurs on a weak or unaccented syllable. The pressus on *-ter-* (Fig. 39) is definitely stressed because *-ter-* is the accented syllable of the word; that on *-la* (Fig 40), however, is slightly stressed since this is the last and weak syllable of the word.

53. Specific notes in some neumes: there are two neumes in which one note is always prolonged: the first note of a quilisma (par. 35) and the second note of a salicus (par. 36). There are two salici and two quilisma in the following examples from the Requiem Introit:

Fig. 42

54. A good example of the frequent occurrence of long notes is found in the Introit of the Requiem Mass given in the above illustration. The note over *Re-* of *Requiem* is long because of repetition; the second note over *ae-* of *aeternam* and over *do-* of *dona* are long because they are the second notes of salici; the first *sol* over *-is* of *eis* and over *-at* of *luceat* are long since they are the first notes of quilisma neumes. The seven dotted notes are clearly shown. In this short selection there are four of the five indications of length. There is no example of the episema, however. In the Offertory of the Requiem Mass (exclusive of the Versicle), to which the student may refer, we have: 23 dotted notes; 5 notes or figures with episema; 4 examples of repetition and 7 quilisma.

Summary

1. The contrast between brief and long notes is very important in the chant (par. 44).
2. The length of notes is slightly influenced by the text and the rhythm (par. 45).
3. An ordinary Gregorian note has the time value of an ordinary syllable in Latin prose (par. 46).
4. The time value of an ordinary note is called the 'basic pulsation' of that melody (par. 47).
5. All notes are practically equal in duration except those marked long (par. 48).
6. The marks of length are: (1) the dotted note, (2) the episema, (3) repetition of the same note over the same syllable, (4) the pressus and (5) the first note of the quilisma and the second note of a salicus (pars. 49-53).

CHAPTER IV

THE NATURE OF RHYTHM

55. In general, rhythm is a movement; specifically, it is a flowing movement. The word 'rhythm' is derived from the Greek word *rhein* which means 'to flow'. Anything that rises and falls in its progress through space, like the waves of the ocean, the flight of a bird, the bouncing of a ball or even the lifting and setting down of the foot in a walk, may rightfully be called a rhythmic movement through space.

56. Because of the similarity of the tones in a melody to the rise and fall in nature, the word is also applied to the movement of music. Every melody is like a flowing body that tends toward a climax and seeks rest after the climax is reached. But such movement in music does not take place through space but in time. In Gregorian chant we are concerned exclusively with melody produced by the voice whose rhythm consists solely in the rise and fall of the tones as they rise towards a climax and fall to rest from it.

57. If, then, a melody is to have rhythm or, in other words, is to be set into a flowing motion, there must be a constant rising or falling in each of its notes. But how is this effect produced in the tones? There are three means especially that create a flowing movement within the melody. If one note is high and the other low in pitch, the one seems to rise and the other to fall, for the rise in any movement is always high and the fall, lower. Then, again, if one note is light and the other, heavy or stressed, the light note leaves the impression that the note is rising and the heavy, that the note is falling, for a rising body is always relatively light and a falling body, always relatively heavy. Finally, if one note is brief and the other long, the brief note seems to rise and the other to fall, since a flowing body never remains long in a suspended position but rises only to fall again. These concepts, therefore, are the three features that produce a rhythmic movement: **pitch, stress and duration.** The first concerns scale tones: the highness or lowness of a note; the second, concerns weight: the lightness or heaviness of a note; and the third, its extent in time: the brevity or length of the note. We shall now examine the character and importance of each.

58. **Pitch.** When a note which is high in pitch is followed by one that is lower, there is conveyed a definite feeling of motion. If we sing 2 1 2 1 2 1, we notice how the rhythm rises on 2 and falls on 1. But we saw (par. 20) that melody and rhythm are interdependent. Can we, therefore, produce a real rhythmic flow when the rise note

is lower in pitch than the fall note? We can if we add another feature to counteract the inversion of pitch. If we sing 1 2 1 2 1 2, making 2 definitely longer than 1, we see how the lower note seems to rise and the higher but longer note seems to fall. The reason lies in the concept that brevity indicates a rise; length, a fall. Melody, then, is very important, but not the most important, feature of a rhythmic movement; if we can invert it, it must not of necessity be essential to the rhythm. Furthermore, we can sense a definite rhythm in the beating of a drum although it is devoid of all melody. There is even a distinct rhythm in the dot and dash of telegraphy. Hence we conclude that, since rhythm can be created without melody, melody is not an indispensable feature of rhythm.

59. **Stress.** In regard to stress, as was stated above, notes also seem to rise and fall when one is light and the other heavy or stressed. A rise note will, of course, always be light, for a body must yield its weight in order to rise. But must a fall note be heavy? We know from experience that when a body falls, it will touch the ground with a stress proportionate to its weight. A rubber ball falls much more lightly than a billiard ball. A ball of yarn falls even more lightly than either of these balls because it is lighter in weight. A snow flake falls to the ground without the least perceptible stress. But a musical tone is even lighter than a snow flake. Its fall must therefore be lighter. Indeed, it is immeasurably light, for the snow flake is after all a material thing of material weight. But no measuring device, however delicate, can determine the weight of a tone. In singing, the tone is made by the breath and lives on the air; the sound we hear is air set in vibration. Modern music bases its rhythm on stress, on the heavily accented beat. But this is contrary to the spirit of the chant. Stress would, indeed, render the rhythm of the chant very clumsy and would steal from it its peaceful flow. Chant melodies as such are without stress; when stress does appear, it comes to them not from the rhythm but from the nature of the text, or the heaviness of the syllable on which a note is sung (see Chap. VIII). From this consideration we deduce a practical hint for singing the chant more beautifully: *the rise notes should be sung lightly and briefly and the fall notes will take care of themselves.* We may apply here the same principle which holds in the material world: an object will fall to the ground of itself but it must be raised by a force outside itself. When we throw a ball into the air, we need not be concerned with its return to the ground. This it will do of itself. Likewise this will be true in singing the chant. The rise notes should be lifted with brevity and the fall notes will fall of themselves. The unwarranted concern about the nature of the fall note lies only in our confusing the chant rhythm with that of modern music. When in the future the fall note is referred to as 'weighty', it should be remembered that 'weighty' is used (a) as a weight proportionate to the weight of a musical tone and (b) as a correlative to the lightness of the rise note.

60. **Duration.** By duration we mean the contrast between brief and long notes. This is the most essential feature of a rhythmic

movement in the chant. The rise note must of necessity be brief and the fall note long or at least comparatively longer than its rise. We have already observed the influence of duration (par. 58) where it produced a real rhythmic flow even when the melody was inverted. The underlying reason for the importance of duration lies in this: that a body always remains at rest until it is brought into motion. If it is raised, it falls to rest as soon as possible after its rise. Furthermore, a moving body rises only to fall again. No one lifts the foot in walking for the purpose of keeping it suspended, but in order to lower it at a more distant point. When the step is completed the foot rests at the fall, never at the rise. We can invert melody, we can dispense with stress, but we cannot invert or dispense with duration and still procure a real rhythmic movement. Duration is the essential feature of a rhythmic movement. A rise can never be long and a fall can never be brief in any natural movement.

61. What happens if we make the rises long and the falls short? We shall have a sort of movement which a lame person executes when he walks. In the case of a person suffering from a severe pain in the foot, if he walks at all, his foot will remain suspended as long as possible. He will lower it only to renew support and then for the briefest possible moment. In this instance the rises (lifting of the foot) are long, and the falls (lowering of it) are brief. This rhythmic flow is neither natural nor beautiful. The nature of rhythm is distorted: the rises are long and the falls brief. In music this kind of rhythm is one which modern musicians call 'syncopation'. There is no place in the chant for such unnatural rhythm. In Gregorian music every rise is brief and every fall is long.

62. We have found that the ordinary notes of the chant are either square or diamond-shaped and that the most common note is the square punctum. But regardless of the shape of the note, all are practically of equal duration unless there is some special indication of length. Yet when we see two notes that are exactly alike in print, for example, two square notes, and when we know from the grouping that the first is a rhythmic rise and the other a rhythmic fall, then the fall note should always be slightly longer than the rise because the essential quality of the fall note is length. That is the reason why every ordinary note has *practically* the same duration. The monks of Solesmes (to whom we owe the recent restoration of the chant), intended to mark some of the notes with a 'c', meaning 'celeriter' or 'quickly', when they first published their rhythmic editions. But because of the objections raised by those who disagreed with them, the authorities at Rome thought it best to exclude these signs. The fact remains, however, that the rise notes are always brief and the fall notes comparatively long. This subject will be treated further in succeeding chapters.

GREGORIAN CHANT

Summary

Elements of rhythm	procured by notes
rise	**high** in melody, **light** in stress, **brief** in duration
fall	**low** in melody, **weighty** in stress, **long** in duration

CHAPTER V

THE DEVELOPMENT OF RHYTHM

63. Rhythm, we have seen, is a movement that flows in a series of rises and falls. We have observed that the essential quality of the rise is brevity and that of the fall is length. We have learned, in other words, that the rise of the rhythm, whether it be high or low in pitch, must be brief in duration, and that the fall, whether high or low in pitch, must be comparatively long in duration.

64. Because every rhythmic movement must consist of at least one rise and one fall and because the rise is essentially brief and the fall essentially long, we should be able now (if the theory is correct) to procure a true and complete rhythmic movement through the agency of a brief and a long note. The brief note represents the rise to action and the long note the fall to rest.

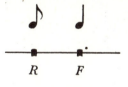

Fig. 43

65. This combination of a brief rise and a long fall constitutes in reality a complete rhythmic movement. It has beginning and end, a rise to action and a fall to rest. One without the other is meaningless and incomplete, but united, the two form an entity which is a complete rhythmic movement. This combination is known as an *elementary* rhythm. It is elementary because it contains only the elements of a rhythm; it cannot be further divided without destroying its nature; it is a complete rhythm because it consists of a rise and a fall.

66. We must study this combination more thoroughly, for in grasping it clearly we shall learn the elements of every rhythmic movement. As a chemist by analyzing one test-tube of water from a lake learns the ingredients of all the water in the lake, so we, by analyzing the smallest possible rhythm, learn the elements of every rhythmic movement.

67. The brief rise note expresses activity and liveliness; it is the beginning of a movement, the transition from the state of rest to the state of motion. The rise note, then, being brief, is the active, lively portion of the rhythmic movement.

68. The fall note, on the other hand, being long, expresses repose and completeness. It is the end of a movement, the return to the state of rest from the state of motion. The fall note, being long, expresses rest and repose and constitutes the peaceful portion of the rhythmic movement.

69. We can see how natural and reasonable this theory is by comparing the rise and fall notes to a step in walking or a word in speech. In taking a step we lift the foot and immediately put it down. The lifting is brief, corresponding to the rise of a rhythm; the setting is long, corresponding to the fall of the rhythm. The former is naturally brief because we lift the foot only to put it down again; the latter is long because the step is completed and ended at that point. In pronouncing a word, for instance, *A-men*, we notice that the first syllable is brief and the last, long. One syllable is comparatively brief because it is the beginning of the word; the other is long because it is the end:

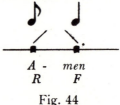

Fig. 44

It is evident that a step would cease to be such if we inverted the order, making the lift long and the setting brief. The foot would remain suspended; anyone witnessing this unnatural movement would grow anxious to know when the act would be completed in a long setting. This is true also with the word. The word *A-men* would be as unnaturally distorted as the step if we rendered the first syllable long and the last, brief:

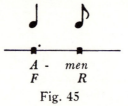

Fig. 45

Furthermore the flow of rhythm of the word is smoothly delineated by the joining of the accent marks, the acute and the grave:

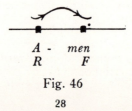

Fig. 46

DEVELOPMENT OF RHYTHM ¶ 70–71

This discussion reiterates and further clarifies the principle: that every rise is brief and every fall is long.

70. Melodies are not composed of a series of elementary rhythms any more than the ocean is considered a composite of waves. In order that the elementary rhythm become a part of the whole, it must lose itself, as it were, within the whole, just as one wave loses itself in the swell of the sea. The rise of each elementary rhythm is, and always will be, brief; but the fall note, while remaining a fall, must sacrifice some of its finality in becoming a part of the whole. Again a comparison with walking may clarify the subject. In taking a single step the foot is lifted and immediately put down: the lift is brief and the support long because it constitutes the end of the step. But in taking a walk of four steps, each of the first three supports, while remaining supports, are not prolonged because the walk is not (but could be) terminated at any of these points. If each support were long, we would hardly consider the series as one walk but rather as four individual steps. In order, then, to unite them into one new element, into a walk, the falls yield some of their length to become a part of the whole. There is no doubt that these supports are not places of permanent rest but rather places of temporary support. In the following figure we show a series of elementary rhythms which, having long falls, do not form a complete entity:

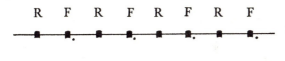

Fig. 47

Each fall implies a separate end of the preceding rise. But in Figure 48 the falls, while remaining falls (but falls of support), sacrifice part of their being to become a part of the whole.

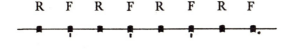

Fig. 48

71. This element may be compared to a word in speech as was done in the elementary rhythm. In pronouncing the word *De-us*, the last syllable will be slightly prolonged because it forms the end of the word. Likewise, if we pronounce the words *Pa-ter* and *Je-su* and *Chri-sti* individually, the last syllable of each will be prolonged because it constitutes the end of each word. But when we join the four words into one continuous phrase, *De-us Pa-ter Je-su Chri-sti*, the last syllables, while remaining the ends of the individual words,

yield some of their length in order to become a part of a new phrase. It is unnatural and incorrect, therefore, to pronounce the four words individually as

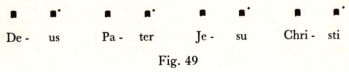

Fig. 49

for in this form they still remain four separate individual words. But when the last syllables give up part of their length while remaining last syllables of words, they form a new entity, one whole phrase. The last syllable of the last word will, however, be long because this syllable is not only the end of the word but the end of the whole phrase as well:

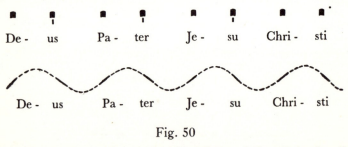

Fig. 50

We observe how readily the flow is delineated if we join the direction of the grammatical accents. We should remember too, for it will serve us to good purpose later, that the so-called 'acute' accent is delineated in an upward movement and the 'grave' accent, in a downward movement.

72. The rhythmic falls of the chant take place on the *ictus* notes (par. 15). The word is derived from the Latin meaning 'thrust' or 'tap'. But we must not be misled into the belief that the Romans 'thrust' or 'struck' these notes as though they were the stressed or heavy or accented beats, like those of modern music (par. 59). On the contrary, the falls in Roman and Greek music were so delicate that an external aid was needed to convey the rhythm to the dancers and to secure uniformity of motion. This aid was supplied by the 'tap' made by the director; hence the use of the word 'ictus'. The ictus, then, is that note on which the rhythm dips down for support during its flow or for rest at the end of the flow. Compared to the flight of a bird, it is that note on which the bird, after opening its wings, closes them to lift itself higher or, on its downward flight, closes them to prevent a sudden drop. If compared with a step in a walk, they are the settings of the foot, with this difference, however: in walking the foot is set with a weight proportionate to the weight of the body, but in the chant the settings are weightless because the flowing element, the melody, is entirely without weight.

DEVELOPMENT OF RHYTHM ¶ 73-74

As has been said above, too much stress should not be laid upon the correct rendition of the ictus notes; after all, if the rise notes are lifted through brevity and lightness, the falls or supports or ictus notes will take care of themselves.

73. In future lessons there will be employed a number of terms to designate this rhythmic beat. It might be called a 'touch,' a 'support', a 'fall' or an 'ictus' note, for all these terms are synonymous. In observing the movements of a bouncing ball we learn an important aspect of the rhythm of the chant. When a ball bounces, the rise before a fall and the rise after that fall merge and become one at the moment of support. In the same way the ictus note is the end of one rise and the beginning of the next. Thus it serves as a unifier of the notes. In point of fact, it is the great unifying force among all the notes of the chant. The rise note is always brief, the fall or ictus, comparatively long; the one is active, the other restful.

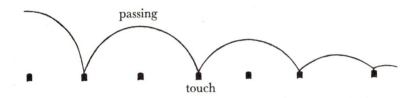

Fig. 51

74. From the above two kinds of rhythmic falls may be distinguished: a fall of support and a fall of rest, one being a fall to a temporary rest and the other to a permanent rest. The first is long in comparison with the rise; the second is long in reality. In our modern conception of rhythm too much emphasis is laid upon the correct rendition of the heavy or accented beats of a measure. Such a procedure may be warranted in modern music, but in the chant we heartily recommend that the rise of the brief note be given our special attention. The rise note is the active portion of the rhythmic movement and its activity lies in the brevity with which it is rendered. In this sense the fall notes of support will be comparatively longer. These falls are always long by nature for two reasons: (1) they descend to the place of rest although they do so only for support; and (2) the rhythmic movement can be ended at any of these points but never on a brief rise note. In practice, therefore, to procure the feel of the rhythm and to insure the rhythmic flow, it is well at times definitely to prolong the falls and to abbreviate the rises; whereupon the notes can be equalized and the rhythmic flow just experienced will be maintained. The greater the contrast of duration, the more definite is the rhythmic flow:

Fig. 52

75. The rhythmic notes may be considered in various combinations:

(1) An elementary rhythm is made up of a brief rise and a long fall of completion.

(2) A simple rhythm consists of a brief rise and a fall of support.

(3) A 'time group' or simply a 'group' of notes consists of an ictus or fall of support with one or two rise notes. This last combination is not a rhythmic group since a rhythm consists of a rise and a fall in that order and not the contrary. For this reason it is not called a 'rhythmic group', but a 'time group' or simply a 'group' of notes.

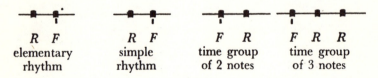

| R F | R F | F R | F R R |
| elementary rhythm | simple rhythm | time group of 2 notes | time group of 3 notes |

Fig. 53

Summary

1. A rise note is essentially brief; a fall note essentially long (par. 63).

2. The combination of a brief note representing a rhythmic rise and of a long note representing a rhythmic fall constitutes a real rhythmic movement (par. 64).

3. The above combination is called an elementary rhythm (par. 65).

4. A knowledge of the essences of an elementary rhythm reveals a clear knowledge of all rhythm (par. 66).

5. The brief rise expresses activity; the long fall expresses repose (pars. 67, 68).

6. The length of the fall of an elementary rhythm is sacrificed for the unity of the whole (par. 70).

DEVELOPMENT OF RHYTHM

7. The rhythmic falls of the chant take place on the so-called 'ictus' notes (par. 72).

8. There are two kinds of fall notes: (1) a fall of support which is long in comparison to its rise and (2) a fall of rest (either temporary or permanent) which is long in reality and generally marked as a dotted note (par. 74).

9. Notes can be combined in various ways:

   (1) A brief rise and a long fall is called an elementary rhythm.

   (2) A brief rise and a fall of support is called a simple rhythm.

   (3) A fall of support and one or two rise notes is called a group of notes: a group of two composed of a fall and a rise, and a group of three composed of a fall and two rise notes. These are called 'time groups' or simply 'groups' (par. 75).

CHAPTER VI

THE PURPOSE OF RHYTHM

76. Rhythm is the soul of a melody. Its presence endows the composition with life and unity: with life in so far as the melody is in a constant state of motion within itself; with unity in so far as the notes are gathered into one whole, sacrificing their individuality and becoming parts of a great movement. What the soul is to the body, rhythm is to the melody. Just as the soul gives life to the body and keeps it from disintegrating, so rhythm gives life to the melody and converts the collection of the many notes into one vital flowing melody. Moreover, no note may ever be deprived of its rhythmic character of a rise or a fall note because as soon as the rhythm ceases, then also will there be a cessation of vitality and unity. The life of a melody consists in its rhythm; rhythm consists of a brief rise and a long fall.

77. When all the notes are gathered into one grand rise and fall movement, each note sacrifices its individuality to become a part of the whole. The note will never lose its identity as a rise or fall note even though it yields its individuality, just as a drop of water is lost in a wave although it never ceases to be what it is. Similarly, words that make up a poem remain individual words even though they have relinquished their individual existence in favor of the whole. When the notes of a melody are unified and vivified through the agency of rhythm, we hear not a series of individual notes but one sweeping melody made up of many notes. We recognize therein, although we may not necessarily know how or why, the delightful pleasure of order, the beauty of composition and the splendor of created life. Where there are life and unity, there also are peace and beauty.

78. In preceding chapters we have analyzed a rhythm to learn its essential elements. From now on we shall concern ourselves with the task of synthesizing the notes; that is, unifying them into a sweeping whole. This is possible only if we know the essence of a rhythmic movement. If all the notes are marshalled under one rise, which must be brief, and one fall, which must be long, then we have succeeded in converting a series of many notes into one new entity: a living, unified whole, one rhythmic movement. In Chapter V we fused two notes into a simple or elementary rhythm. In Chapters VII and VIII we shall combine the notes into groups. In Chapter IX the groups will be united into musical divisions and in Chapter X the divisions will be united into complete musical phrases, the largest of all divisions. These are the means whereby the purpose of rhythm is achieved.

PURPOSE OF RHYTHM

Summary

1. The purpose of rhythm is to form a complete whole of all the notes of a melody (par. 76).
2. When notes are united into one whole the selection is endowed with life and unity (par. 77).
3. Our present task consists in uniting all the notes of a selection in one complete whole (par. 78).

CHAPTER VII

THE UNITING OF NOTES IN NEUMATIC CHANTS

79. Every note of a melody is either a rhythmic rise or a rhythmic fall note and as such is a member of a group of notes.

80. Every group of notes is made up of an ictus or fall note (pars. 72, 75) and one or two rise notes. While the ictus note is naturally the end of every rhythmic movement, it is considered the first of every *time group*. In other words, the ictus or fall note forms the unit according to which notes are grouped. This procedure is both practical and theoretical: it is practical because the ictus is the outstanding note of a rhythm and the note at which the rise notes are fused (par. 73); it is theoretical because the ictus is in reality the end of a rhythmic movement though considered here as the beginning of a group.

81. No ictus note may ever follow another ictus note directly. This is reasonable for a moving (or flowing) body must rise after each fall in order to prepare for another fall.

82. One rise note must follow a fall or ictus note; two rise notes may follow an ictus note. A group which is made up of one ictus and one rise note is called a 'time group of two notes' or simply a 'group of two'; a group which is made up of one fall note and two rise notes is called a 'group of three' notes:

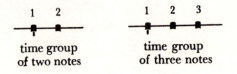

time group of two notes   time group of three notes

Fig. 54

83. In modern music the rhythm is regular in the sense that the rhythmic flow descends for support at regular intervals. In modern $\frac{2}{4}$ or even $\frac{4}{4}$ time, the rhythm supports itself regularly in groups of two's; in modern $\frac{3}{8}$ or $\frac{3}{4}$ time the rhythm falls regularly in groups of three's. In the chant, on the other hand, the rhythm is free in that it descends for support in groups of both two's or three's.

UNITING OF NOTES IN NEUMATIC CHANTS ¶ 84-86

Modern music

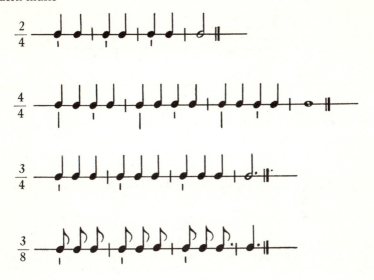

Gregorian rhythm

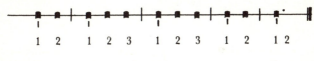

Fig. 55

There is no set standard for the sequence of groups since the rhythm of the chant is born of and built upon the freedom of Latin prose in which groups of two's and three's follow each other indiscriminately.

84. In grouping notes in a Gregorian melody, then, (1) every note belongs to a group of notes of which the ictus is always the first; (2) no ictus may follow immediately one upon another ictus; (3) no ictus may carry more than two rise notes. The grouping of notes in modern music is clearly expressed by the time signature, bar lines and the time value of the notes. The grouping in the chant, however, is determined according to fixed principles.

85. The grouping of notes in neumatic chants is established by the neumes. The law for neumatic grouping may be expressed as follows: the first note of every neume is the ictus. There are two exceptions to this law: (1) when the second note is definitely marked as the ictus (par. 15); (2) when the second note is long.

86. In regard to the first exception, the second note in a neume may be marked as the ictus in order to produce a certain rhythmic effect. In this case the first note loses the ictus quality.

Fig. 56

If the third note of a neume, however, is marked, the first note may still retain the ictus quality.

Fig. 57

In regard to the second exception that the ictus is not on the first note of a neume if the second note is long, there are two considerations: (1) the second note is always long (and always marked with the ictus) in a salicus (par. 36); (2) the first note loses the ictus when the second is fused into a long note by the pressus (par. 52). These are illustrated in the following figure:

separate neumes

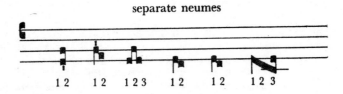

pressus

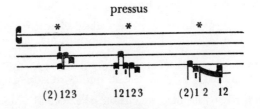

Fig. 58

UNITING OF NOTES IN NEUMATIC CHANTS ¶ 87

Ictus and length are so closely associated that the first note of all length is always the ictus note except when the second note is marked with the ictus (this happens rarely):

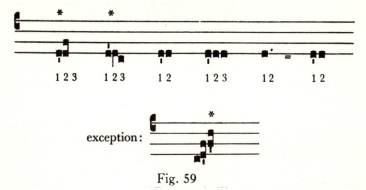

Fig. 59

In the case of the pressus, three conditions must be present: (1) the last note of one neume and the first of the next must be in unison; (2) they are printed close together because (3) they are to be sung on the same syllable. For example, in Figure 42, we can observe how the separate neumes are spaced when they are distinct and how close together they are when the notes form a pressus.

87. We have seen that no note may ever stand alone or that every note belongs to a group. But what happens to notes that are separated or isolated from their neumes or that stand alone between neumes?

Fig. 60

Such notes become members of the preceding group. If the preceding group is made up of two notes, the isolated note recedes and becomes the third of that group (Fig. 61 [a]); if, however, the preceding group is made up of three notes, the isolated note divides the four into two groups of two's (Fig. 61 [b]):

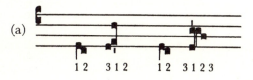

Fig. 61

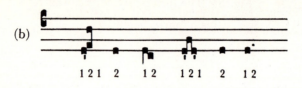

Fig. 61 (cont.)

88. Sometimes a melody or new phrase begins with a single note. Such a note cannot stand alone and yet there is no preceding group to which it can attach itself. In the case of a new phrase the isolated note cannot recede to the last group of the previous phrase since the phrase mark indicates completion (par. 12 [b]). In such cases a rest must be supplied. This rest functions as a silent ictus.

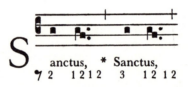

Fig. 62

The use of the rest is practical inasmuch as a melody or phrase may begin with either a rise or a fall note. Very often when the text begins with an accented syllable, the chant delights in setting that syllable to a rise note in order to give it its proper lightness. This nuance in turn lends an active beginning to the phrase.

89. When an incise or a member begins with an isolated note, that note follows the same rule of recession as described above (par. 87), since neither incise nor member implies completeness (12 [c], 12 [d]). The following sections of the Requiem Offertory illustrate the foregoing rule:

Fig. 63

UNITING OF NOTES IN NEUMATIC CHANTS ¶ 90

90. An analysis of the grouping of the first phrase of the Requiem Introit is given in Fig. 64. The letters above the staff refer to the rhythmic groups of two and groups of three. Notes marked with arrows indicate isolated notes which recede, becoming members of the preceding groups.

Fig. 64

- a First note of length
- b Four notes divided into two groups of two's
- c Last syllable of word (see next chapter)
- d Marked as ictus
- e First note of length (pressus)
- f Dotted notes
- g First notes of neumes

Summary

1. A group of notes is made up of an ictus and one or two rise notes (par. 80).

2. No ictus note may follow another ictus note directly (par. 81).

3. Rules for Grouping Notes in Neumatic Chants (par. 84 ff):

    (a) A note is the ictus or first of a group if it is so marked (par. 85).

    (b) The first note of every neume is the ictus unless the second note is marked or long.

    (c) An isolated note recedes and becomes a member of the preceding group. If the preceding group is composed of two notes, the isolated note becomes the third; if the group is made up of three notes, the series is divided into two groups of two each; if it is made up of more than three notes, the ictus will be placed on a virga (if it occurs) or on an important note of the mode.

    (d) If the isolated note begins a new phrase or a new melody (in which case it cannot recede to a preceding group), a silent ictus is supplied as the first note of that group; the isolated note becomes the second note of the group and the group is counted *rest* 2.

CHAPTER VIII

THE UNITING OF NOTES IN SYLLABIC CHANTS

91. In syllabic chants there are few, if any, neumes (par. 19 [a]). Just as the grouping of the neumatic chants is determined by the neume (par. 85), so the scheme of grouping for syllabic chants is based upon the nature of the syllables of the text. Our present task is to learn which syllables will most naturally support the rhythmic ictus. This note, as in the neumatic grouping, will be the first of every group. The same principles apply now as before: no ictus may succeed another immediately; every group is composed of one ictus and one or two rise notes (par. 85).

92. In order, then, to render the chant in its original purity, we must learn to respect the Latin word as it was pronounced in the days when the melodies were composed. The character of the melody and the flow of the rhythm (pars. 20-23) are to a great extent based upon the nature of the words in the text.

93. Syllables are unified into words through the agency of rhythm; that is, through a rise and fall movement. We know that a rise and fall movement may be procured by means of pitch, stress and duration (par. 57). In Cicero's time (about the beginning of the Christian era) duration was the governing principle, especially among the cultured. But among the unlettered the principle of melody was maintained only until about the 11th century. From that time on, stress gradually took the place of melody. This last change dealt the death blow to the Latin language as a popular language and gave birth to the modern Romance languages of Italian, French and Spanish. It is to be remembered that the syllables were equal in duration and were rhythmized according to the agency of melody during the golden age of the chant.

94. When melody was the principle of rhythmizing syllables into words, all syllables were largely of equal duration. The rise and fall were procured by a gradually ascending pitch on the syllables preceding the accent and a gradual descent in pitch on the syllables following the accent. Although the feature of melody thus became pre-eminent, still it was impossible to drop entirely the other two features of rhythm. The gradual rise in pitch was accompanied by a gradual increase in volume (crescendo) and the descent in pitch was accompanied by a decrease in volume (decrescendo). Furthermore, the feature of duration was retained, although in the form

UNITING OF NOTES IN SYLLABIC CHANTS ¶ 95–96

of a slight hastening of tempo (accelerando) before the accent, and a slight slackening of tempo after it (rallentando).

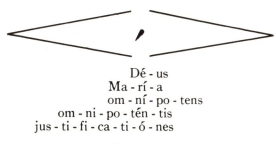

Dé - us
Ma - rí - a
om - ní - po - tens
om - ni - po - tén - tis
jus - ti - fi - ca - ti - ó - nes

Fig. 65

95. The accented syllable, as can readily be seen, is without doubt the most important syllable of the word. It forms the turning point of the rhythmic movement by determining the end of the rise and the beginning of the fall movement. It is the climax, the highest part of the word, and seems to draw the syllables to itself (by the increase of volume and tempo) and to restrain those after it (by the decrease in these elements). In this way the syllables of every word are unified and vivified into one new being.

96. In the correct rhythmization of the chant the accented syllable is very important and yet little understood today. First, there is not the least implication of stress in the original meaning of the word 'accent'. It is derived from the Latin words *ad* (to), and *cantus* (sung), and implies something melodious. The words were later contracted to *accantus*, and still later changed to *accentus*. Today when we speak of an 'accented' syllable or an 'accented' beat, we always think of something 'stressed' or 'emphasized by pressure'. This concept formed no part of the original meaning of the word 'accent' and must form no part of our interpretation of the chant. It must be remembered, therefore, that the syllable was, and for us who desire to sing the chant correctly still is, the 'sung' or 'melodious' syllable of the word. Secondly, it is pre-eminently the high syllable of the word since it forms the end of the rise and the beginning of the fall in the rhythm of the word. Although it is essentially high in melody, it partakes nevertheless of the other qualities of the rise; namely, it is also light and brief. At about the 11th century this syllable became lengthened and stressed; this treatment, as was said, was one of the factors that gave birth to the Romance languages. The opposite of the 'accent' or high syllable is naturally the low or 'grave' syllable, from the Latin *gravis* (heavy) whence came the French '*grave*' meaning 'low'. But when the accented (the *adcantus*) syllable became stressed, it was called the 'acute-accent' syllable. And so today we speak of the 'acute' and the 'grave' accents. Here, however, is a confusion of terms: a syllable cannot be both grave and accented since 'grave' implies 'lowness', and 'accent', 'highness'. Henceforth, therefore, in order to

keep before the student this basic difference, and at the same time to be more accurate in regard to the chant, the terms 'accented' and 'grave' will be employed only in reference to syllables. The accented syllable, often termed the 'tonic' or 'primary' syllable, can also be regarded as the rise syllable, the grave as the low or fall syllable of the word.

97. In regard to the position of the accent in Latin, all words divide into two kinds: spondee and dactyl. The spondee is a word whose accented syllable is next to the last syllable:

Dé - us
Ma - rí - a
de - pre - ca - ti - ó - nes

The dactyl is one whose accented syllable is the second from the last:

Dó - mi - nus
om - ní - po - tens
ju - sti - fi - ca - ti - ó - ni - bus

98. In addition to the primary accent, longer words also have secondary accents. These are found on every other syllable, counting back from the primary accent, in both spondees and dactyls:

p = primary accent   s = secondary accent

Spondees	Dactyls
s s p	s s p
6 5 4 3 2 1	7 6 5 4 3 2 1
ad - ju - ván - dum	ad - ju - tó - ri - um
re - ve - re - án - tur	ma - gni - fi - cén - ti - a
su - per - ex - al - té - mus	de - pre - ca - ti - ó - ni - bus

99. Now we are prepared to analyze the nature of syllables to determine on what syllables the rhythmic ictus can most conveniently fall. In view of paragraphs 69 and 71(q.v.), the most natural place for the ictus is the last syllable of words. There are four reasons: (1) the last syllable, being the end of the word, is most naturally low, long and weighty, having the same characteristics as the ictus note (par. 72); (2) it is most natural that the end of the word should correspond with the end of a rhythm rather than the beginning; (3) the contrary treatment, that is, the agreement (in quality) of the last syllable with a rise note which is naturally high, light and brief (par. 96) would violate the very nature of the word; (4) the last syllable will naturally be a final rest if this is the last word of the text. The last syllable of a word, moreover, will be a fall because it is the end of a word; the fall will be qualified, however, and will be less long when the word is not the last in the text.

100. Since rhythm has a law of its own apart from the text (pars. 20 - 23), it does not happen invariably that the rhythmic ictus or fall note coincides with the last syllable of words. But since

the rhythm should respect the nature of the word as far as possible, we do find that most words have the ictus on the last syllable. It is quite evident that when the last syllable of a word is set to a rise note of the rhythm (that is, when it is pronounced in such a way that the last syllable is high, light and brief), it cannot be styled 'natural'. Consequently, a word has its natural rhythm when the last syllable coincides with the ictus or fall note; if not, it is deprived of its natural rhythm. This rule has been attacked on the ground that if the ictus is on the last syllables of the text, those last syllables are 'accented' or 'stressed' — a treatment which mutilates the Latin word. But those who propose this objection fail to realize that the ictus note is not a stressed note; it is rather the fall of a rise note and as such it need not necessarily be heavy (par. 59). In the Offertory of the Requiem Mass there are 52 words of more than one syllable. Of these, four are definitely deprived of their natural rhythm.[1]

101. In rhythmizing chants, if the ictus is placed on the last syllable whenever possible, some ictus will be made to support more than two notes. Syllables other than the last syllables must be found to carry the ictus.

102. If we allow a spondee its natural rhythm by placing an ictus on the last syllable, the accented syllable cannot have an ictus, for two ictus notes cannot stand side by side:

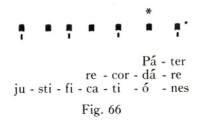

Pá - ter
re - cor - dá - re
ju - sti - fi - ca - ti - ó - nes

Fig. 66

Hence the accent of a spondee generally occurs on the rise note of the rhythm. In other words, in a spondee the accent and ictus **alternate**. Sometimes, however, the chant will set a neume on the accent. In this case the ictus and accent **coincide**:

om - ni - po - tén - tis

Fig. 67

---

[1]The four words are: *libera* (first), *fidelium, profundo, morte*. (See Fig. 79.)

103. If we allow a dactyl its natural rhythm the word accents can also carry the ictus:

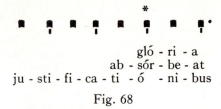

Fig. 68

As if to allow both rhythm and text their independence, the chant will sometimes place a neume between the accented syllable and the last syllable in a dactyl, thus removing the ictus from the accent:

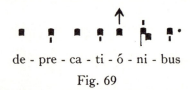

Fig. 69

This is particularly true of the *special dactylic cadences* which are explained in the chapter on Psalmody (par. 212).

104. We have noted that the ictus is placed on alternate syllables, counted back from the last known ictus. But we know also that the secondary accent is placed on alternate syllables, counted back from the primary (or last) accent (par. 98). The rhythm will, therefore, always be the same:

Fig. 70

In the following figure we shall see what happens to the different accents when different types of words are set to this rhythm:

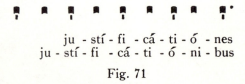

Fig. 71

In spondees the ictus and accent alternate; that is, the ictus will occur on grave syllables. [In other words, the accents of spondees occur on rise notes, the accents of dactyls occur on fall (or ictus) notes.]

UNITING OF NOTES IN SYLLABIC CHANTS ¶ 105-107

105. What is the importance of this consideration? Herein lies one of the most charming features of Gregorian rhythm and one of the fundamental principles of the theory of Solesmes. In modern music the word accent is made to fall always on the heavy beat of the rhythm. The monks of Solesmes state that rhythm and text are independent of each other; that the ictus may or may not occur on the accented syllable. The importance of this principle lies in this fact: the accent of the word is always high, light and brief (par. 96); the fall of the rhythm is always low, long and weighty (par. 68). Definite phenomena appear when the accent occurs on the rise and when it occurs on the fall note.

106. When the accent of the word occurs on the rise note of the rhythm, we have concurrence of two like forces; the lightness of the accented syllable of the word and the lightness of the rise note of the rhythm. Because the most important feature of the rise is brevity, such a note must be sung with particular brevity; it must be brief both because of the rise note of the rhythm and because of the accent of the word. We may compare this rendition to the effect of a ball thrown upward by a smart toss of the hand; the hand represents the rhythmic rise and the ball represents the word accent. Both rise together but the quicker the toss of the hand, the higher the ball will rise. This movement can be pictured by joining the accent marks of the syllables and by indicating the crescendo and decrescendo to and from the accent:

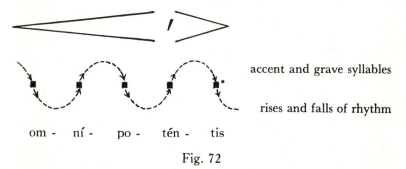

Fig. 72

In such a rhythm the flow leaps **over** the accents of the words.

107. When the fall of the rhythm occurs on the accent of the word, we have a contention of two opposing forces; the accent of the word will always be high, light and brief, while the fall of the rhythm must be low, long and weighty (par. 68). How can these two opposing forces be reconciled on an identical note? The answer is: by stressing the accented syllable. This and the pressus are the only cases where the fall note of the chant is heavy or stressed (par. 59). The reason for the stress is that the accent of the word must be lifted. The example of the hand and the ball can illustrate the effect. The hand again represents the rhythm and the ball, the accent. If the ball is thrown downward with definite pressure, it will rebound upward from the floor. The more forceful the downward thrust, the higher will be the rebound. In this way both elements are satisfied. We may note the progress in this delineation, observing that there is a double action on the same note:

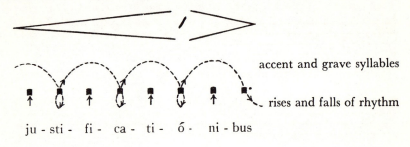

Fig. 73

In such a rhythm the flow **leaps upon** the accents of the word.

108. It is well to treat the secondary accents of the words in the same way as the primary accents whenever possible; that is, if the primary accent is on the rise note, the secondary accent or accents should be set to rises when possible. This will insure the similarity of accents in the same word.

109. This peculiarity of the ictus and accent, in one case co-inciding and in another alternating with each other, lends a definite charm to the chant. While ordinary rise notes are high, light and brief, those rise notes set to the accents of words are especially high, light and brief or, rather, higher, lighter, and briefer than the others. In the same way an ordinary fall is low, long and weighty, but a fall on the accent is lower, longer and weightier than an ordinary fall. In other words, the accents of words magnify the qualities of the rhythm. We cannot fail to see how the composers have diligently tried to vary the accents in all of the chant selections, at times even achieving a perfect balance within the selection. In examining the *Pange lingua* (Mode III) we note how the accents of one division are on the ictus while those of the others are on the rise or off the ictus. We shall consider secondary accents as we do the primary accents (which indeed they would be if the words were shorter); monosyllabic words will be compared with longer words of a corresponding line of the hymn. There are twenty accents:

UNITING OF NOTES IN SYLLABIC CHANTS ¶ 110–111

Fig. 74

Accents on rise notes (12)

Pán	- ge		lín	- gua				
Sán	- gui	- nís		- que	pré	- ti	- ó	- si
Frú	- ctus		vén	- tris	gé	- ne	- ró	- si
Réx	ef	- fú		- dit				

Accents on fall notes: (9)

gló	- ri	- ó	- si			
Cór	- po	- rís		mys	- té	- ri - um
Quém in		mún	- di		pré	- ti - um
gén	- ti	- um.				

In the first line two accents coincide with the ictus, two alternate; in the second line all accents coincide with the ictus; in the third line, all accents alternate; in the fourth line, all accents coincide with the ictus; in the fifth line, all accents alternate; in the sixth line, one accent coincides with the ictus and the other accent is off the ictus. This peculiarity can hardly be laid to chance; it was undoubtedly the wish of the composer to vary the accents.

110. Two places have already been found for the ictus in syllabic chants: (1) on the last syllable of words; (2) on the accents of dactyls. In rare cases when these principles do not suffice or when there may be a choice, the ictus will be preferably placed on melodically low notes rather than on high notes since the ictus is naturally low and long.

111. Thus far we have considered the natural rhythm of the word. The melody, however, also affects the word (par. 93). It is the nature of the Latin word to be pronounced with a slight rise in pitch to the accented syllable and a slight descent in pitch from it

(par. 93). When the melody therefore respects the word in such a way that it places on the accented syllable a note higher than that of the last syllable, we say that word has its natural melody. It may happen at times, however, that the melody rises and in so doing it will ascend even if higher notes are set to last syllables. For example, in the Requiem Mass the melody treats the first two *Sanctus* differently from the third. On the third the melody climbs in such a way that the last syllable is higher than the accented syllable:

Fig. 75

The first two *Sanctus* are treated naturally in respect to the rhythm and melody, but the third is deprived both of its natural melody and its natural rhythm: of the natural rhythm, because it lacks an ictus on the last syllable; and of the natural melody, because the last syllable is higher than the accented syllable.

112. What practical value has this consideration? When a word is deprived of its natural melody, it is often well to deprive it of its natural rhythm. This is advisable because in this case the accent becomes stressed and it seems to lend the proper downward pressure needed before an ascent. Before a person can jump up from the floor, he must prepare himself for the upward spring by a downward pressure. This pressure is supplied by the heavy accent. Of course the voice is different from the body; it needs no spring before an ascent. On the other hand, the chant is so calm and natural that it requires no more of the voice than nature demands of the body. In another example, the beginning of the *Salve Regina*:

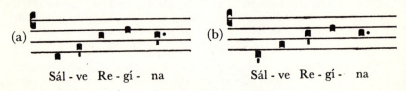

Fig. 76

we observe how clumsily the rhythm rises at (a) in which we give the word *Salve* its natural rhythm by setting an ictus on the last syllable. But at (b) the ictus is set to the accent which renders the accent stressed. In the first figure the word has its natural rhythm; in the second figure it is deprived of its natural rhythm because it is deprived of its natural melody.

UNITING OF NOTES IN SYLLABIC CHANTS ¶ 113

113. At times it will be either impossible or inadvisable to give each word its natural rhythm. In such cases, since the last syllable has more claim to the ictus than the accent, words should be given their natural rhythm, whenever possible, by setting an ictus on the last syllable:

Two dactyls: nó - mi - ne   Dó - mi - ni

rather than: nó - mi - ne   Dó - mi - ni

Fig. 77

Yet the rhythm of the chant is sufficiently free to allow the director a choice. For example, in the last verse of the *Dies irae*, the words *Pie Jesu, Domine, dona eis requiem*, could be rhythmized as at (a) below:

(a) Pi- e Jé-su Dómine, dóna é- is réqui- em.

(b) Pi- e Jé-su Dómine, dóna é- is réqui- em.

Fig. 78

In this way each word is given its natural rhythm. The rendition at (b), however, seems preferable for these reasons: 1) the heavy accents on the words *Pie Jesu Domine* lend a definite seriousness to the last prayer of the long sequence; 2) these accents, being heavy, form a delightful contrast to the many light accents throughout the selection, especially those of the first and like verses; 3) if the words *Pie Jesu* were given their natural rhythm, the dactyl *Domine* could not support an ictus on the accent although it is almost needed for ascent on the last syllable (par. 107). However, as was said, either choice is equally correct; the very freedom of the chant gives to the individual director the freedom of choosing what appears to him best in each case.

¶ 114. As an exercise in finding which words have their natural rhythm and which their natural melody, we can examine all the words of the Requiem Offertory:

UNITING OF NOTES IN SYLLABIC CHANTS ¶ 114

Fig. 79

* Words having natural melody but lacking natural rhythm
** Words having natural rhythm but lacking natural melody

There is a total of 52 words having more than one syllable; 4 of these have their natural melody but their unnatural rhythm, and 10 have their natural rhythm but unnatural melody. The remaining 38 are treated as natural from the point of view of both rhythm and melody.

Summary

1. The rhythm of syllabic chant is based on the nature of the syllables of the text (par. 91).
2. The accented syllable is the highest part of the word (par. 95).
3. Spondees have the accent on the next to the last syllable; dactyls have it on the second syllable from the last (par. 97).
4. The most natural place for the rhythmic ictus is on the last syllable of a word (par. 99).
5. A word whose last syllable carries the ictus is said to have natural rhythm (par. 100).
6. Spondees cannot support an ictus on the accented syllable (par. 102). Dactyls generally can (par. 103).
7. When the accent of a word occurs on the rise of the rhythm, that accent is especially high, light and brief (par. 106).
8. When the accent of a word occurs on the fall of the rhythm, that accent is especially low, long and weighty (par. 107).
9. A word is said to have its natural melody when the accented syllable carries a higher melodic note than the last syllable (par. 111).
10. In cases of doubt, and where these rules are not sufficient to supply the place for the ictus, it is well to remember that the ictus is preferable on low rather than on high notes (par. 113).
11. Whenever possible, the secondary accents of words are to be treated in the same way as the primary accent (par. 107).

CHAPTER IX

THE UNITING OF GROUPS OF NOTES

115. In the two preceding chapters we united individual notes in neumatic and syllabic chants into groups consisting of an ictus and one or two rise notes. The process of unification will now extend to the forming of the groups into rhythmic movements.

116. Just as every note is either a rise or a fall note (par. 79), so every group is either a rise or a fall group.[1]

117. The first note of every group is the ictus note. The ictus note is a rhythmic fall either of support or of rest (par. 73). This note may fall for support in order either to rise higher or to enjoy a temporary rest. The flight of the bird illustrates these elements. A bird whose destination is a high mountain peak will soar up to the peak not in a straight line but in a series of curves necessitated by the opening and closing of its wings. Each closing will bring the bird higher, but each closing will also necessitate a reopening. At the reopenings, therefore, the bird will lose altitude and will descend somewhat until the next closing. Thus, the closing of the wings corresponds to a rise group in rhythm, the reopening to a fall group. On descending from its destination the bird will repeat the same process with this difference however: the openings will be the more important part of the flight; the wings will be closed only to break the force of gravity and to make the fall more smooth.

118. The rise group has, therefore, the qualities of the rise note: it is high in melody, light in stress, and especially brief in duration. The fall group, correspondingly, possesses the qualities of the fall note: this is low in melody, weighty in stress, and especially long in duration. The term 'weighty in stress' is used in relation to 'lightness in stress' of the rise note. Although the rise group is indeed light, the fall group is not arbitrarily "heavy", only relatively "heavier" than the rise group. The rise group is the active, lively group while the fall group is its restful counterpart.

119. Which groups will, therefore, be rendered as rise groups and which will be rendered as fall groups? The following is the general rule: after the syllable of the word is satisfied, the melody determines the nature of the groups. Whenever possible,[2] the accented

---

[1] In many texts on chant rise and fall are termed respectively *arsis* and *thesis*. For the sake of practical clarity the author prefers the terms *rise* and *fall group*.

[2] The qualifying condition, "whenever possible," is suggested for on occasion the melody disregards the nature of the syllable since text and melody are not governed by the same principles. When, therefore, an important climax occurs on the last syllable of a word, that particular group of the climax will be rendered as a rise regardless of the nature of the syllable. Notice the important climax on the last syllable of *eis* and *luceat* in the Requiem Introit.

syllables will be rendered as rise groups and the grave syllables as fall groups. This is done to satisfy the nature of the syllable (par. 94). But when the nature of the syllable has been satisfied, the grouping will follow the flow of the melody in such a way that ascending melodies will be rendered as rise groups and descending melodies as fall groups. Finally, the first group on the primary accent of a word will always be rendered as a rise and the last syllable as a fall—for the rise group is to the rise note what the fall group is to the fall note (par. 117). The following is an analysis of examples from the Requiem Mass:

(a) **Kyrie**:

Fig. 80

Analysis:
    Groups 1 and 2: rise groups — rising melodies on accent of word.
    Groups 3 and 4: fall groups — falling melodies on last syllable.
    Group 5: rise group — a secondary accent of the word.
    Group 6: fall group — a grave syllable of the word.
    Group 7: rise group — the primary accent (this ictus is slightly stressed).
    Group 8: fall group — the last syllable of the word.

(b) **Gradual**:

Fig. 81

Analysis:
    Groups 1 and 2: rise groups — on accent of the word.
    Group 3: fall group — the grave syllable of the word.
    Group 4: fall group — the last syllable (from here the melody rules).
    Groups 5, 6, 8 and 9: rise groups — the melody ascends.
    Groups 7, 10, 11 and 12: fall groups — the melody descends.

120. Further analysis of the nature of groups will finally establish the general principle that *one group grows out of the other*. One rise group which follows another will be a more marked rise than the first and will be slightly more active; likewise, one fall group following another fall will be a more marked fall and will be slightly more restful. Furthermore, whenever a fall group follows a rise group, that fall will constitute a slight repose from the preceding rise. An example may serve to make the principle and its application clearer. When we ascend a mountain we may sit down along the way for temporary rest. We sit down not at the foot of the mountain but at various points in our ascent. And so upon descending, we rise from the place where we rested. Similarly, in regard to the groups, the rise group which follows a rise is slightly more pronounced because we are nearer the climax. A fall that follows a rise grows out of that rise; that is, it is a slight repose from the rise out of which it has grown. In summary, the rhythm of the chant is never abrupt: one group calmly and smoothly grows out of the preceding.

121. One rhythmic group grows more active or becomes more reposeful than the preceding through the aid of rhythmic features known as *dynamics* and *agogics*. By dynamics is meant the gradual increase or decrease of volume or of loudness and softness. This is indicated in modern music (and can also be applied here) by means of the opening and closing *dynamic angle*:

Fig. 82

The dynamic angle opens to the highest note on a primary accent of the word. Each rise group that precedes this accent grows, as it were, toward it and each group that follows it fades away into silence from it. In the Requiem Mass, for example, the melody treats the word *Kyrie* most naturally:

Fig. 83

UNITING OF GROUPS OF NOTES ¶ 121

Group 2 is slightly louder than group 1; group 4 is slightly softer than group 3; group 3 is slightly softer and more reposeful than group 2. By agogics is meant the gradual increase or decrease of tempo designated in modern music by the words *accelerando* and *rallentando* respectively. In the chant this takes the form of a very slight increase in tempo before the accent and a very slight decrease after it. The reason for the change in tempo lies in the fact that rhythm is a movement. There is a rise to the climax (the accent of the word in the above example) and a fall from it to a state of rest. The rise seems to convey the feeling of a gentle anxiety to reach the destination (the accent) and the fall, the calm enjoyment of having reached it. In this way the word is rhythmized by its groups. The rhythmizing by groups can be compared with the example in par. 119. Each word is given, whenever possible, its proper rise to the accent and fall from it. A further example from the Requiem Mass can be found in the following:

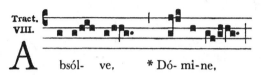

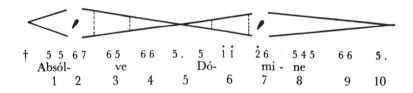

Fig. 84

Summary

1. Every group is either a rise or a fall group (par. 116).
2. The word and the melody determine the nature of the group in this way:
   (a) Accented or rise syllables will, as far as possible, be accorded rise groups (par. 118).
   (b) Grave or fall syllables will, as far as possible, be accorded fall groups (par. 118).
   (c) After the nature of the syllable has been respected, the melody will rule in such a way that ascending groups will be rendered as rises and descending groups, as falls (par. 119).
3. Dotted notes will, in the majority of cases, be rendered as a fall group since the fall group corresponds to the fall note (par. 116).

---

†NOTE: the notation in the above illustration and in the following chapter have been transcribed into numerals so that the student may have a more graphic picture of the rhythm.

CHAPTER X

THE UNITING OF GROUPS INTO DIVISIONS AND OF DIVISIONS INTO PHRASES

122. Chapters VII and VIII presented the combining of individual notes into groups. In the preceding chapter (IX) the groups were organized into their rise and fall movements according to their position on the syllables of words. In this chapter the process of unifying the notes will be extended by unifying the words into musical divisions. Incises will be united into members and members into phrases. Since the phrase is a complete entity in itself (par. 12), the process of unification must end with the unifying of the phrase.

123. Each note must always retain its character as a rise or a fall note and each group must likewise preserve its qualities as a rise or a fall group. Consequently each division will preserve its character of rise or fall. However, each of these simple or compound parts will contribute its share to the rise and fall movement of the whole phrase. As each word in a poem expresses its own idea and yet loses itself in the context, so each note, each group, each subordinate division (incise and member), retains its individuality but is lost within the structure of the whole phrase. And just as a note sacrifices its length to become a part of the greater whole (par. 70), so each subordinate division sacrifices its length to become a part of the phrase.

124. Each subordinate division of a phrase has its own rise and fall movement. The rhythm will rise to a climax in that division and fall to rest from it. The *climax* of a division is generally the highest ictus note on an accented syllable. When the melody ignores the nature of the word, the climax may be set to the last syllable of a word (see the two phrases of the Requiem Introit). But in the more ornate selections, the climax is strictly melodic. In these cases the particular kind of notes used will readily reveal the climax (par. 32). For example, in the Requiem Gradual, the bivirga over the last syllables of *Domine, perpetua,* and *mala* indicate without doubt the melodic climaxes of their respective melodies.

125. An analysis of the first phrase of the Requiem Tract will serve to clarify the theory of unifying members and incises into phrases. The phrase, the text of which is *Absolve, Domine, animas omnium fidelium defunctorum* is divided:

phrase
{
  1st member { 1st incise: *Absolve*
                   2nd incise: *Domine*
  2nd member { 3rd incise: *animas omnium fidelium*
                   4th incise: *defunctorum*

126. The **first incise** consists of one word whose accent is on the syllable *-sol-*. Both melody and rhythm respect the nature of the word in that both rise to the accent and fall to rest from it. The notes are grouped as follows:

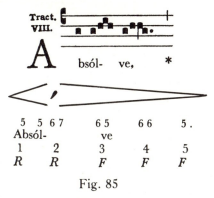

Fig. 85

Considered apart from the whole, this incise will rise from silence and fall to rest in silence. The climax is found in Group 2, the ictus of which is stressed slightly because the ictus and the accent of the word coincide (par. 107). Groups 1 and 2 are rendered actively as rise groups and the others reposefully as fall groups. Groups 3 and 4 become increasingly more reposeful (par. 120) to Group 5 which is the end of our present division. Such repose or falling to rest is expressed by two elements of rhythm, namely, slowness in time and softness in volume. Groups 3, 4 and 5 grow slower and softer in such a way that Group 5 vanishes away slowly and softly into silence. It should be noted that the syllables *-sol-* and *-ve* begin on the rise notes of their groups:

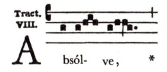

Fig. 86

If we extract these syllables from their context, we find that the *-sol-* and the *-ve* are accorded a simple rhythm since the second note of each is an ictus, the first being a rise note (par. 75). This binds the syllables of the word very closely for each syllable begins on the rise or last note of the preceding group. We should note also how the melody falls from *la* to *ti la* on the syllable *-sol-* and from *la* to *la sol* on the syllable *-ve*.

127. The **second incise** consists of the word *Domine* whose accent is on the first syllable. Here again both the rhythm and the

¶ 128

melody respect the nature of the word. The notes are grouped as follows (again for purposes of analysis each incise is considered distinct from the whole and as an entity in itself):

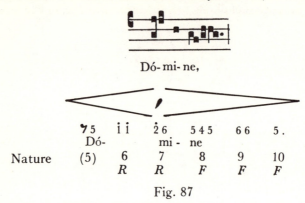

Fig. 87

A rest is supplied for the ictus on Group 5 because this note is isolated by the on-coming pressus (par. 88). This word, considered apart from the whole, begins at silence and falls to rest into silence. Groups 5, 6 and 7 are active rise groups; groups 8, 9 and 10 are restful falls. The syllable *Do-* begins on a simple rhythm. The syllable *-mi-* is rendered on one rise note. This is quite brief and should not be prolonged unduly.

128. The **first member** then consists of the two first incises, *Absolve, Domine*. The end of the first incise will sacrifice its length and its return to silence in order to become part of the whole. When considered apart as a plain incise, it ended in a long fall to silence. Now, however, it neither descends into silence nor is its end as long as before; here it is but a temporary fall for support in preparation for the rise on the next incise. The first *sol* of the *Domine* has become a part of the last dotted *sol* of *Absolve* (par. 87). The two incises could not be more intimately bound together, for the first note of *Domine* is really a part of the last group of *Absolve*. A group of three is formed by the dotted *sol* and the isolated *sol*, the new syllable beginning on this note (see par. 138).

Fig. 88

UNITY OF PHRASES ¶ 129–130

The climax of the whole member is the *re* of the accented syllable *Do-*. The climax of the first incise now drops down to the level of a secondary accent of the member. Since the ictus note *re* of Group 7 is the climax, it receives a slightly stronger stress than the ictus of Group 2 which has now become a secondary accent.

129. The **third incise** is syllabic in character. It contains only two neumes (two podatus): one on the accent of *animas*, the other on the accent of *fidelium*. Since the accent on *fidelium* is the climax of the incise, it will receive a slightly stronger stress than that of *animas*. The incise is grouped as follows:

á-ni-mas ómni- um fi- de- li -um

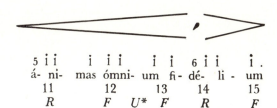

5 i i	i i	i i	6 i i	i .
á- ni-	mas ómni-	um fi-	dé- li -	um
11	12	13	14	15
R	F	U* F	R	F

Fig. 89

Here are three dactyls, each possessing its natural rhythm (ictus on the last syllable, par. 99). But a variety of accents is offered: the words *animas* and *fidelium* have neumes on the accents and must therefore be stressed, but *omnium* has its accent on the rise note of Group 12. The majesty of this incise is displayed by the three groups of three's (Groups 11, 12 and 14). Group 11 is clearly an active rise group; Groups 12 and 13 are fall groups of support in preparation for the climactic accent on Group 14 whose ictus is definitely stressed There must be a constant, almost eager, rise to this accent. Furthermore, each note is of equal value except the last; for this reason there may be no tarrying or hurrying on any syllable.

130. The **fourth incise** consists of the word *defunctorum* whose accent is the syllable *-cto-*. The melody and rhythm respect the nature of the word. In grouping we must remember that the first note of length is always an ictus, for pressus abound in this short incise. The fourth incise is grouped as follows:

---

* U stands for *undulation* (see par. 133).

¶ 131-132 GREGORIAN CHANT

i i	7 2 3	i i	6 i	6 6 5	6 5	i i	6 i	5 5	4 .
defun - ctó-			rum						
16	17	18	19	20	21	22	23	24	25
F	R	F	F	F	R	R	F	F	F

Fig. 90

The climax of this incise is undoubtedly Group 17 on the accented syllable. Group 16 is a fall for reasons explained in par. 139; Group 17 is the climax because of the high melody and its position on the accented syllable. Groups 18 and 19 are falls, the first because of the lower melody, the second because of the last syllable. Group 20 is preferably rendered as a fall because of its length and because it prevents too high a rise on the secondary climax of Group 22. But Group 21 is a rise preparing for the secondary melodic accent of Group 22. The succeeding groups are falls, each helping to bring the phrase to a peaceful end.

131. The **second member** consists cf two incises, one of which is syllabic, the other melismatic (par. 19). The primary climax of the member is Group 17; Group 14 of the first incise is now relegated to secondary importance. The member begins actively on a stressed ictus, descends for a support on Groups 12 and 13 to prepare for the secondary climax on Group 14 whence it falls for another support on Group 15. Group 16 is preferably rendered as a fall of support to prepare for the grand climax on Group 17. The rhythm now falls towards the end of the word but rises quietly again on Groups 21 and 22. These are but secondary rises which break the monotony of the falls. In uniting the two incises, Group 15 is not long and does not return to silence: it is simply a fall of support preparing for the accent on Group 17. (See Fig. 91 on the insert.)

132. The **whole phrase** is, therefore, made up of four incises which are condensed into two members. Each incise and each member is distinct from the other by its own rise and fall movement. This distinction is brought out by brief rises and long falls which distinction is, as was stated in paragraph 65, the very essence of all rhythm. The term 'brief rise' to the climax and 'long fall' from the climax may best be described as 'active beginning' and 'restful end', respectively. Incises, being the least important of all divisions, are accorded active rises to the climax and a slight decrease in volume and speed in the fall from the climax. Members, on the other hand, being more important divisions, are accorded active rises but more pronounced decrease in volume and speed in the fall from the climax.

The phrase, however, rises consistently from the first note to the primary accent (in this example on Group 17) and falls consistently to rest from it. In this sense the first incise in the example given above can be considered as a rise division preparing for the rise in the second incise but without losing its own fall to rest which now becomes a secondary fall of support. The member is brought to a temporary rest of support on Groups 8, 9 and 10. The third incise can be considered as a fall division in which the melody gains momentum, as it were, for the grand rise of the phrase on Group 17. Henceforth all the groups fall to rest but rise groups (Groups 21 and 22) are inserted to break the monotony of the fall (in the eight succeeding groups). Too much emphasis cannot be laid upon the importance of the active beginnings of every division. Just as the life of an elementary rhythm lies in its active rise note, so the life of every division lies in its beginning or rise to the climax. While the ends of the divisions are often rendered slowly and softly, the importance of the beginning is overlooked. The active beginning is as important, if not more important, than the restful end. Each division, as a division, has a right to its own active rise and restful fall even though it loses a part of its individuality in favor of the whole phrase. If breath must be taken in the course of the phrase, the interruption must be so made as not to imply an end (see par. 12). Finally, the last two or even three groups of every phrase are sung very slowly and gradually tapered off into silence. (See Fig. 92 on the insert.)

133. Group 12 is a fall group that contains an accented syllable. The rise note on the accented syllable *om-* of *omnium* is more than an ordinary rise (see par. 107). The special treatment given to this note is called *undulation*, derived from the Latin word *unda* meaning 'a wave'. It is rendered particularly brief; in fact, it is the briefest of all the notes in the phrase (par. 44). It is brief as a rhythmic rise and brief because it is sung to an accent syllable of the word. The undulation occurs only in a fall group which is followed by another fall. This is reasonable for if a rise group were to follow, this note could not be lifted and the rise group could not be respected, for nothing can rise twice without an intermediate fall. Undulating rhythm is further illustrated in the following paragraph.

134. The grouping of a phrase in a syllabic chant can be studied in the *Dies irae,* from the point of view of the climax, of the nature of groups, and of the accents. (See Fig. 93 on the insert.)

(a) In regard to the **climax:** The melody in the first and third members is very sober, giving hardly any indication of its highest point. In these cases the accent of the last word is chosen as the climax. The second member contains a neume on an accented syllable which is undoubtedly the climax of this member as well as of the whole phrase.

(b) In regard to the **nature of the groups:** There are ten fall groups in the total of fourteen groups. Such a condition would render the selection very calm and almost lifeless, were it not for the fact that the rise note of most of these groups is set to an accented syllable. This fact gives each rise definite life (par. 106). The accents of Groups 2, 3, 4, 5, 10 and 11 are undulated over rise notes (par. 133). The reason that these groups must be rendered as falls lies in the fact that the ictus of each is on the last syllable of a word (par. 119).

(c) In regard to **accents**: All the accents of words except one are set to a rise note of the rhythm, thus giving the phrase, as was said, sufficient vitality to counteract the calmness of the many falls. The one accent which has the ictus and is therefore stressed, is the accent of *saeclum* which also forms the climax of its own member as well as of the whole phrase.

135. Careful examination of the two analyses given above will reveal that the goal set at the beginning of the process of unification has been attained: we have marshalled all the notes of one phrase into one grand rhythmic movement—one rise and one fall. Each note, each group and each incise and member while retaining its individual character of a rise or fall, becomes a part of the grand rise and fall of the phrase. The individual groups and divisions have become a part in the uninterrupted flow of rhythm from the beginning to the end of the phrase. Through the agency of rhythm we have unified the notes into one living, flowing rhythmic movement.

136. We have now succeeded in unifying (and by unifying also vivifying) the notes of a complete phrase. The whole process may be illustrated in the scheme in Fig. 94 on the insert.

Summary

1. The process of unification must be continued until all the notes of one phrase are united into one rhythmic movement (par. 122).

2. Each note, each group of notes, each incise and member will retain its characteristic quality of a rise or fall entity although this quality is somewhat sacrificed in deference to the whole phrase (par. 123).

3. Each division retains its own rise to a climax and fall from it (par. 124).

4. A practical example of unifying is given in paragraphs 124-133.

5. When an accent syllable occurs on a rise note of a fall group, which group is followed by another fall group, that note is undulated (par. 133).

6. Syllabic chants are treated in the same way as neumatic chants, as is to be observed in the example given in paragraph 134.

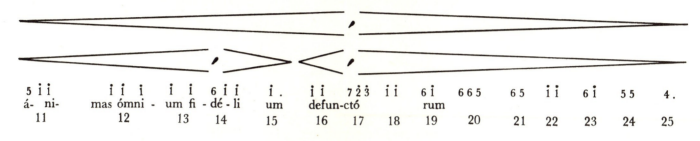

Fig. 91

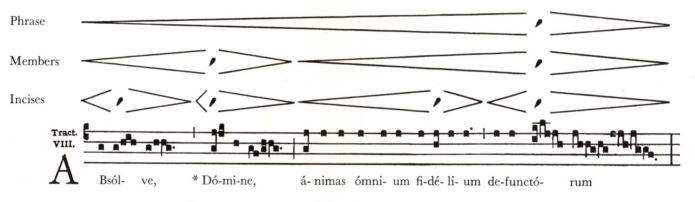

Fig. 92

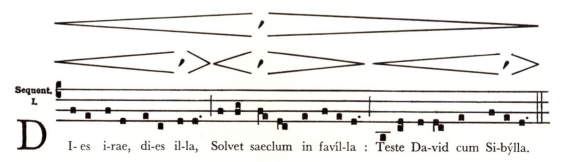

Fig. 93

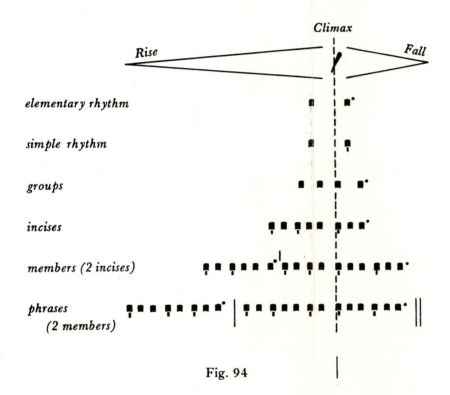

Fig. 94

CHAPTER XI

THE JOINING OF DIVISIONS

137. The principles to be set forth in this chapter were already hinted at and referred to in the preceding chapter. But in order to enlarge upon them and to set them in good order, a new chapter is devoted to their exposition. This chapter, then, will treat of how one division is joined to another. One phrase is never joined to the next since the phrase indicates a melodic and, in the majority of cases, also a textual completeness. Incises and members are, however, joined in a more or less intimate fashion.

138. The most intimate of all joinings takes place when the first note of one division is **isolated** and recedes to become a member of the last group of the preceding division. In this case the end of one division and the beginning of the next are fused into one group. There is an example of this most intimate joining in the first two incises of the Requiem Tract which was discussed fully in the last chapter. Group 5 of Figures 85 and 87 is a time group of three notes, the first two of which are the dotted note and the end of the first incise and the third of which is the isolated *sol*, the beginning of the second incise. This kind of joining can of course be made only when the second division begins with an isolated note. If it begins with an ictus note, that note is the first of a new group which in turn will be either a rise or a fall group.

139. When the second division begins with an ictus note, that note is the first of a group. The next most intimate joining would take place if that group could be rendered as a fall group continuing the fall of the preceding division. The third and fourth incises of the Requiem Tract can be joined in this way. There is no reason why Group 16 in Figure 92 cannot be rendered as a fall. The melody here does not lie higher than that at the end of the previous incise. Objection might perhaps be raised that the ictus note is on a secondary accent (*de-* of *defunctorum*). But that need not change the interpretation for one who prefers to render the group as a fall. For this reason it was suggested (par. 131) that Group 16 be considered a fall group—such a treatment would bind the two incises intimately.

140. The third and least intimate of all joinings takes place when the second incise or member begins with an ictus note which is the first of a group that must be rendered as a rise. In Fig. 92 this happens in the third incise or, in other words, at the beginning of the second member. Group 11 is a rising melody on an accented

syllable; hence it cannot be considered in any way except as a rise group. It is quite evident that this kind of joining is the least intimate, for the last group of one division must of necessity be a fall group while the first of the next division is a rise group on an accent. There is such a difference in the nature of the two that in rendition there must be no doubt as to where one division ends and the other begins. Group 11, beginning the second member, is like the return swing of a pendulum, whereas the other joinings are all within the same swing of the pendulum.

141. In paragraph 137 it was stated: "One phrase is never joined to the next since the phrase indicates a melodic and, in the majority of cases, also a textual completeness." The phrase always indicates a melodic but it may not always indicate a textual completeness. The first phrase of the Requiem Gradual is complete in regard to its melody and text. The words of the first phrase, *Requiem aeternam dona eis, Domine*, express a complete idea and the melody ends on the final of the mode. But the second phrase consists of the words, *et lux perpetua*, which do not express a complete idea. The idea is only completed when the words of the third phrase, *luceat eis*, are added. Hence, if the text is preferred to the melody, there ought to be no interruption at the phrase mark between *perpetua* and *luceat*. But if the melody is preferred to the text, an interruption, that is, a retard and a gradual descend into silence with a pause of two beats before the next phrase, is to be made. The director should use his discretion in such rare cases.

Summary

1. Although all divisions of a phrase are unified into one phrase, one division may be joined more or less intimately to the next (par. 137).

2. The most intimate of all joinings takes place when a division begins with an **isolated note** which becomes a member of the last group of the preceding division (par. 138).

3. The next intimate joining consists in rendering the **first group** of the next division as a **fall group,** continuing the fall at the end of the preceding division (par. 139).

4. The least intimate of all joinings takes place when the **first group** of a new division must be rendered as a **rise group** (par. 140).

5. In rare instances where the text is not complete at the end of a phrase, the text or the melody may be given preference according to the discretion of the director (par. 141).

CHAPTER XII

APPLICATION OF THE PRINCIPLES OF RHYTHM TO SPECIAL FIGURES

142. The principles of rhythm of the foregoing chapters can be applied to special figures where they can reveal delicate and beautiful nuances which might perhaps be lost if attention were not directed to them.

143. In passages where syllables are adorned with single neumes, it is at times difficult to impart a definite rhythmic flow. A hint of sluggishness might characterize the flow in passing from one syllable to the next. Whereas the first note of the neume is generally the fall note, the second (or third, in a group of three) is a rise note and the rises are particularly brief. Therefore, any tarrying on last notes of neumes would have the effect of prolonging the rise notes, robbing the notes themselves of their liveliness and brevity and in turn destroying the very nature of Gregorian rhythm. The beginning of the Requiem Offertory versicle offers an example. For illustration and clarity, the length of the notes can be exaggerated in order to insure an unmistakable rise and fall movement; that is, the rise notes should be sung quite briefly and the fall notes quite long. This section has been transcribed into modern notation (Fig. 95) to show more clearly the variety of length.

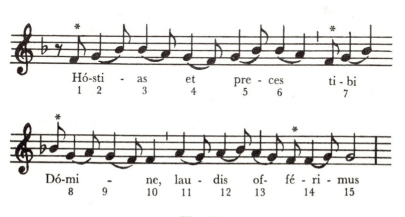

Fig. 95

All the fall notes are given the value of a quarter note, the rises are represented by eighth notes. Rendered in this way, the rise of the rhythm on the brief notes and its fall on the long notes are clearly felt. All word accents are sung to the rise notes of Group 1, 6, 7 and 13. These notes are particularly brief because of the accent. The ictus of Groups 5 and 11 are stressed. This passage (or any passages that might lack rhythm) should be sung as written over and over again until the rhythm is definitely felt; the notes should be given their time value as called for in the chant notation and the flow will be insured.

144. For practice, in order that the student feel a true rhythmic flow, it was recommended that rise notes be abbreviated and fall notes prolonged. Frequently, however, this very device is indicated by the notes themselves: the fall note is lengthened by an episema, by repetition or by length in the neumes. In the Requiem Offertory the following are found:

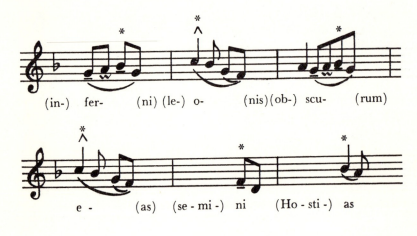

Fig. 96

On the syllable *-i* of *perfrui* at the very end of the Requiem Tract we find a four-fold repetition of the rhythmic figure:

Fig. 97

In the above illustration it will be noted that the falls of each rhythmic figure are definitely prolonged in order to guarantee the rhythmic flow. Notice how the flow is insured on the syllable *-tu-* of *beatitudine* in the Requiem Tract:

RHYTHM AND SPECIAL FIGURES ¶ 145

be- a- ti- tú-

Fig. 98

The first and second *la* are long to lift the *sol* that occurs between them. In the *Dies irae* (third stanza) there is a melodic inversion of five notes; that is, the rhythmic fall is five notes higher than the rhythmic rise:

Li-ber scriptus pro- fe-ré-

Fig. 99

In spite of the melodic inversion, the rhythm is guaranteed if the fall note is lengthened as indicated and the rise note rendered briefly as usual.

145. The episema (pars. 16, 50) indicates that the note (or notes) over which it stands is to be prolonged slightly beyond its ordinary length. A fall note is long by nature; the episema will extend its length to a slight degree. A rise note is brief by nature; the episema will prolong it slightly. In other words, the episema does not render all notes over which it appears equally long: it merely extends their natural length. Furthermore, the groups that appear at the beginning of incises and members are quite active and brief; those at the end are by nature restful and long. The episema will give slight prolongation to each. The *Kyrie* of Mass I furnishes an example. In the *Christe* of that composition there is a torculus with episema on the accent of the word. This torculus is quite brief by nature since it occurs at the beginning of the division and on an accent of the word. The episema prolongs the torculus somewhat. But there is also a torculus with episema on the last syllable of the second *Kyrie*. This torculus is naturally long because it occurs on a last syllable and near the end of the division. Again the episema prolongs its value somewhat. But there is a vast and pronounced difference in time value between the two: the first is quite active even with the episema, the other very restful because of it.

Fig. 100

146. The rise notes of the chant are rhythmically brief but are not all of the same brevity. The third note of a group of three is slightly briefer than the second because it is a more definite rise than the second. Furthermore when an accent occurs on that third note, the lift of the accent renders it even briefer (see third note of rise in Groups 5, 9, 10, 13, of Fig. 93). There are nine instances in the Requiem Offertory, including the three already mentioned, in which the accent of a word (either primary or secondary) occurs on the third of a group.[1] (See Fig. 79.)

147. The chant delights in 'leaps' on and off a syllable. The leap is brought about by setting the notes on a syllable in such a way that the first is brief, the second long and the third brief. The first represents the spring, as it were, upon the syllable; the second, the momentary settling upon it; the third, the leaping off to the next syllable. These leaps may occur in an ascending or descending melody. The salicus (leap) is generally used for the upward leap. The two syllables *ae-* of *aeternam* and *do-* of *dona* of the Requiem Introit are so treated. The *lu-* of *luceat* and the *non* of the Gradual are similarly treated. The *Do-* of *Domine* of the Tract is leaped upon but here the effect is produced by the pressus. Sometimes it is the pressus that makes the downward leap, as with *-ter-* of *aeternam* in the Introit. The *-ter-* of the *aeterna* in the Gradual versicle is leaped upon, as shown by the ictus on its second note. But such a settling on the syllable is not as long as when represented by the pressus. Of course, when the leap is on an accented syllable, the settling is stressed. In the Introit the *ae-* of *aeternam* and the *do-* of *dona* are

---

[1] The words are: *Christe, libera* (first), *Abrahae, promisisti* (secondary accent), *tibi, Domine* (second), *offerimus, eas* (last), *Domine* (last).

adorned with the salicus. The ictus of the first is long, of the second, both long and stressed because the first is on a weak syllable of the word, whereas the second is on the accented syllable.[1]

148. The first note of length takes the ictus (par. 84) except when the second is marked as ictus. Although the latter occurrence is relatively infrequent, it does appear in the Requiem Gradual and in other Graduals similar to it. In the Requiem Gradual on the last syllable of the last word, *timebit*, there is found this rhythmic figure:

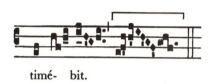

timé- bit.

Fig. 101

Transcribed into modern notation, it appears as follows:

Fig. 102

In order to insure the correct rendition of this nuance, we must prolong the notes that are marked long (designated by an asterisk) and render the others quite briefly. But we shall observe that two *do's* are adjacent, the first being brief and the other long. The only way to distinguish one from the other is to alight briefly but delicately upon the first and, by a slight repercussion (a delicate interruption of breath), to sustain the second.

149. In paragraph 120 we learned that one group of notes grows out of the other. This is especially true where there is little variation in melody. In other words, in passages where the melody contributes little or nothing to the rhythmic flow, other features of dynamics and agogics must be called upon to help bring it about. Each group in these sections is exaggerated in its rise or fall qualities. So, for instance, in the third incise of the Tract there is very little variety of melody (Fig. 89). But if each group is given definite dynamic qualities, the rhythm must become evident. Thus, a beautiful melody

---

[1] The student may examine these compositions for himself in the figures which have been given in the preceding chapters.

¶ 150

like that on the *ju-* of *justus* in the Gradual would become stagnant unless the dynamics were emphasized. That melody is transcribed below with the rhythm indicated.

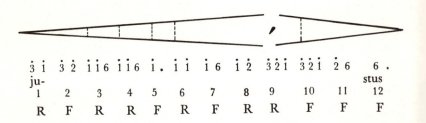

Fig. 103

In this short passage, groups are repeated. Groups 3 and 4 are alike in rhythm and melody; Groups 5 and 6 differ only in notation (one a dotted note, the other a repeated note); Groups 9 and 10 are alike in melody. But rhythmically, that is, dynamically, they differ: Group 9 is louder and faster than Group 10. Group 4 is louder and more active than Group 3 because the former is nearer the climax; Group 10 is softer and more restful than Group 9 because the latter is the climax and the former prepares for the fall. The difference in dynamics is indicated in some degree by the vertical dotted line that appears within the dynamic angle. Unless the differences in rhythm and melody are made evident, beautiful passages such as the one illustrated here will be deprived of their inherent beauty. Without rhythm they can have no life or unity.

150. In paragraph 119 it was stated that ascending melodies are to be rendered as rise groups and descending melodies as fall groups. Moreover, rise groups are active because they are rendered briefly and fall groups are restful because they are rendered comparatively longer. This introduces the feature of spirituality into the chant. This concept is often difficult to understand for we are too accustomed to think of heavy things rising slowly and falling fast and light things, on the contrary, rising fast but falling slowly. The ascending melodies are rendered as active rise groups and the descending melodies as reposeful fall groups and as such never to be hurried.

151. As the dynamic angle opens and closes very gradually, so do the dynamics of the chant increase and decrease gradually. The transition in volume from one note to another or from one group to another, is never abrupt or sharply defined. It is a bad habit among singers to render the higher notes louder than the lower. In the chant this habit is intolerable. In the Requiem Gradual the syllable *-is* in the phrase *luceat eis* finds its climax on high *fa* but the rise to it is very gradual. So also the transition from the second to the last incise on the syllable *-ter-* of *aeterna* (from *la* to high *re*) must be performed in a very delicate fashion. The *la* forms a fall group which is indeed quite soft but the next high *re* should not be much louder. In chant nothing must divert the perfect calm from the flow of the melodies. They reflect the "peace that the world cannot give", that is sought and found in the House of God.

152. It has been maintained throughout this book that the beginnings of divisions are active and the ends are reposeful. Activity without repose implies haste but, contrariwise, repose without activity reflects sloth. A temperate mixture of both must be introduced in every division. There seems to be no difficulty in rendering the end of a division reposefully. But the beginning of the next division must be imbued with new life. Care should be taken, therefore, to begin each new division actively. Where this is not done, the tempo decreases gradually to such a degree that the phrase loses its life long before it should descend to rest. In the Requiem Tract, therefore, the word *Absolve* is ended rather peacefully but the next word *Domine* is a new beginning which must reflect activity. Likewise the new member *animas omnium fidelium* begins in a lively manner and falls to a temporary respite on its last syllable, but the beginning of the next word *defunctorum* is full of life since it forms the climax of the whole phrase.

GREGORIAN CHANT

Summary

1. Delicate nuances more thoroughly explained (par. 142).

2. Syllabic chants are enhanced by careful rendition of rise notes (par. 143).

3. Lengthening fall notes and abbreviating rise notes often brings out the rhythm (par. 144).

4. The episema. slightly lengthens the note or notes which it effects (par. 145).

5. Rise notes are not all of the same brevity (par. 146).

6. The chant delights in leaps (par. 147).

7. When the second note of length has an ictus, a slight repercussion is necessary in its rendition (par. 148).

8. Dynamics are employed to procure rhythm when the melody fails (par. 149).

9. When rising groups are rendered actively and fall groups reposefully, the chant is invested with a definite spiritual character (par. 150).

10. Dynamics in the chant are always smooth (par. 151).

11. Active rises and restful falls cloth the chant with life without rush, and rest without sloth (par. 152).

CHAPTER XIII

DIRECTING THE CHANT

153. The directing of the rhythm of the chant by hand is called *chironomy*, a word derived from the Greek words *cheir*, meaning 'hand' and *nomos*, meaning a 'usage' or 'direction'.

154. Chironomy depicts the rhythmic flow of the individual notes and of note groups, and also indicates the volume levels at which the group is to be sung. It delineates the individual notes in so far as the hand is always in a relatively lower position on the first note of each group than on the second (or third in a group of three). The first note of the group is the support note from which the second (or third in a group of three) rises. The group is represented by curves made upward from right to left (for a rise group) or downward from left to right direction (for a fall group). The dynamics are represented by the height at which that group is described.

155. The simplest form of rhythm consists in an alternation of rise and fall notes. An example of this form is the simple *Dies irae* where the rises occur on the accents and the falls on the final syllables. The hand is raised and a curve described from left to right like an inverted U over the accented syllables and lowered on the ictus notes. This is more familiarly known as *undulating rhythm* (par. 133). The rise notes are on the accents but in fall groups. The hand movement finds its origin in the nature of the syllables as found in the form of accent signs. This undulating movement has already appeared in joining the accent marks of the words as in Fig. 46. In describing this form of rhythm the hand is lifted lightly but briskly in a curved motion over the accent syllables or rise notes and is allowed to drop of its own weight on the last syllables. The restraint implied in the words 'drop of its own weight' suggests that the ictus on weak syllables is never stressed.

156. The next simplest form of chironomy consists in an alternation of rise and fall groups. This form is quite rare since the melody is hardly ever content to move in so regular a fashion. It is found, however, in the *Adoro Te*. In this kind of rhythm the hand is raised in a curved upward line from right to left for the rise groups and in a downward curved line from left to right for the fall groups. A rise group of three is delineated in a larger curve, the hand being highest at the count of three; a fall group of three is described in a larger downward curve, the hand, in this case, too, being highest at the count of three. It is important to note that in every group the hand is lower at the count of *one* than at the count of *two* (or *three* in a group of three).

157. The most common of all rhythmic formations consists in an indiscriminate succession of rise and fall groups. It is to be noted that when one rise group is followed by another, the junction of the two groups will be delineated in a small circle described upward from the left and downward to the right. The upward movement describes the one or two rise notes of the preceding group while the downward movement depicts the ictus of the second group.

158. When one fall group follows another, the hand is raised in a rather horizontal curve describing the one or two rise notes of the first group and allowed to drop gently to depict the ictus of the next group.

159. It is to be understood, of course, that the hand does not progress in space as notes do on paper. Very little space is needed to delineate the figures as represented in the last illustration. In any case, the hand need never extend beyond the dimensions of the body. The chironomy in the monastery at Solesmes is so unobtrusive that no one is aware of the choirmaster's direction since he stands with his back to the congregation. It is said that he uses nothing but the wrist and index finger for even the most emphatic kind of direction. Such a procedure, however, presupposes great skill on the part of not only the director but the singers as well.

160. The director should not lay too much emphasis on grace of the chironomy. At the final performance it is the director's duty to start his singers together, to keep them together throughout, and to bring them to the finish together. Any other instructions should be given them prior to their appearance and should be practiced during the rehearsals. Furthermore, some directors execute the most graceful chironomy while the minds of the choir members wander and their eyes are fixed on some foreign object. Other directors need only to chironomize in a calm and unobtrusive fashion: the rendition is good because they have the attention of their choir. Whatever signs of direction are used, they are good if they are understood by the choir. An attentive, well-schooled choir needs very few of them.

Summary

1. A rise group is delineated in an upward curve beginning at the right and bearing towards the left; a fall group is delineated in a downward curve beginning at the left and bearing towards the right (par. 154).

2. The undulation is described by a brisk curve made in an upward and downward motion over the accent to be lifted (par. 155).

3. In delineating a group the hand is always lower at the count of one (the ictus note) than at the count of two; in describing a group of three the hand is raised higher on the count of three than on the count of two (par. 156). This is true of both rise and fall groups.

CHAPTER XIV

THE APPLICATION OF GREGORIAN PRINCIPLES TO MODERN MUSIC

161. In applying the foregoing principles of Gregorian rhythm to modern music, it should be noted that the modern system of notation, while practical in itself (especially since the introduction of polyphonic music) does, however, detract from the true nature of rhythm.

162. Every rhythm in modern music is severed into measures by the bar line. No measure is a natural unit or complete entity in itself. The last note of every measure is the first note of a rhythm and the first note of every measure is the last note of a rhythm. This has been brought about by setting the bar line before the original ictus note. But the ictus note is really the fall or end of the rhythm. The bar line or the divisions of the notes into measures is merely a convenience for setting the rhythmic beats in strict mathematical order.

163. In modern music the first note of every measure is the 'accented' beat and as such represents the fall of the rhythm. It necessarily follows that the last note of every measure is the light or 'unaccented' beat and as such represents the rise of every rhythm. But it has already been demonstrated (par. 68) that the fall or 'accented' beat is in reality the end of every rhythmic movement and the 'unaccented' beat is the beginning of every rhythmic movement. In modern music, however, rise and fall notes, or the 'unaccented' and 'accented' notes are unnaturally placed at the end and at the beginning of each measure respectively. Thus the bar line divides, or rather breaks up, every simple rhythm.

164. An example of this apparently confusing (but in modern music, practical) method, will clarify the exposition. In paragraph 71 the simple phrase *Deus Pater Jesu Christi* was used to show the most natural place for the rhythmic ictus (i.e. on the last syllable of the words):

Fig. 104

If the phrase were set in modern measures, the bar lines would be placed before the ictus:

Fig. 105

Every word is thereby divided. Of course, the moderns could never tolerate such a treatment because the fall note in modern music is invariably considered as the 'accented', the **stressed** beat. It is entirely out of the question to stress the last syllable of Latin words. Hence, the next best place for the rhythmic beat was on the accented syllable. And there is where it is invariably found today. But in Gregorian chant the fall is not necessarily heavy or 'accented' but long (par. 60). There is, therefore, no contradiction nor distortion in setting the ictus on the last syllables in the chant.

165. The word accents are generally set to the accented beats of the measure. This renders every accent heavy (since it concurs with the fall of the rhythm). This may account for the change in meaning of the word 'accent' from its former implication of *melodious* to its more modern meaning of *stressed*. In modern rendition one syllable of a word is often assigned to the end of a measure and the other syllable to the beginning of the next. Thus again the bar line bears no relation to the rhythmic flow. Examination of the simple yet popular *Lullaby* of Brahms with the usual English text demonstrates how words and measures are dislocated:

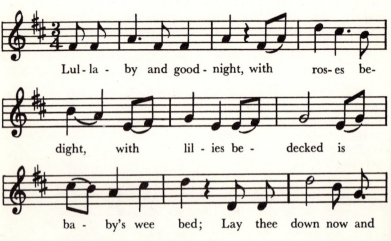

Fig. 106

GREGORIAN PRINCIPLES AND MODERN MUSIC ¶ 166

Fig. 106 (cont.)

166. Modern music uses the whole note as its unit of measure. Every other note is a fraction of this note.

Fig. 107

In vocal music certainly it would be more practical and rational to consider a shorter note as a unit. A shorter note would better express the time value of a syllable in discourse (par. 46). If in practice the the eighth note were considered the unit, many rhythmic difficulties would soon be solved: all the rhythmic units of the larger note could then be broken down into their proper value and the rhythmic elements of each could readily be recognized:

Fig. 108

Furthermore, shorter notes would add life to the movement, for in the longer notes the rhythm can easily be lost. If we realize that there are eight movements in a whole note, the rhythm must of necessity continue to flow:

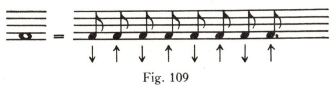

Fig. 109

167. Even though modern music bases its rhythmic principle on stress, it cannot deny the importance of duration. The last notes of each measure are brief (because they are rhythmic rises) and the first notes are long (rhythmic falls). In the Lullaby (Fig. 106), in only one case (from measure 2 to 3) is the rise note almost equal in time value to the fall (par. 44):

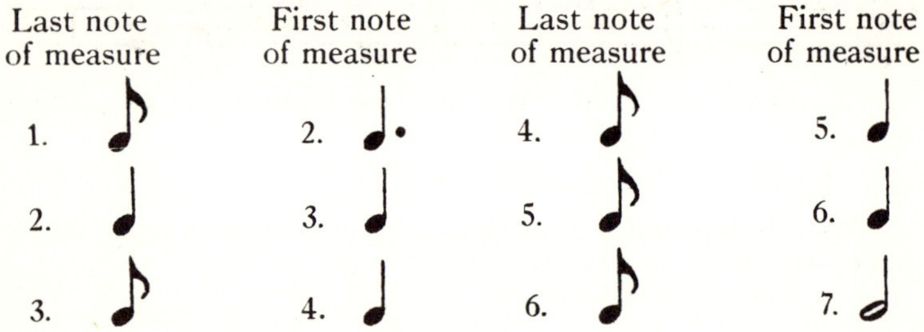

Last note of measure	First note of measure	Last note of measure	First note of measure
1. ♪	2. ♩.	4. ♪	5. ♩
2. ♩	3. ♩	5. ♪	6. ♩
3. ♪	4. ♩	6. ♪	7. ♩

Fig. 110

168. The larger musical divisions are seldom designated. There are no subordinate divisions to indicate the structure; they must be inferred from the text and its meaning, from the music and its organization. It can be said that in general every sentence of text with its setting corresponds to a musical phrase in the chant. It can be broken up into subordinate divisions according to the structure of either the sentence or the musical phrase. Each of these subdivisions must possess its own rise and fall, subordinated to the sentence according to the principles laid down in Chapter X. The Lullaby can then be divided and subdivided as follows:

1st phrase
   1st member
      1st incise: Lullaby and good-night
      2nd incise: with roses bedight
   2nd member
      3rd incise: With lilies bedecked
      4th incise: is baby's wee bed.

2nd phrase
   3rd member
      5th incise: Lay down now and rest
      6th incise: May thy slumber be blest
   4th member
      7th and 8th incises: repetition of 5th and 6th

The dynamics can be represented as follows:

Lul-la-by and good-night, with roses bedight,

Fig. 111

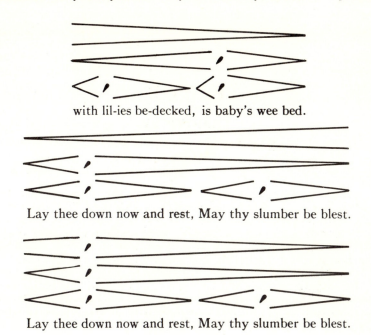

with lil-ies be-decked, is baby's wee bed.

Lay thee down now and rest, May thy slumber be blest.

Lay thee down now and rest, May thy slumber be blest.

Fig. 111 (cont.)

169. In the simple rhythms of $\frac{2}{4}$, $\frac{3}{4}$ and $\frac{3}{8}$ time there is one ictus to each measure, occurring on the first beat. In the compound rhythms, however, such as $\frac{4}{4}$, $\frac{6}{8}$, etc., there are two ictus notes, a primary and a secondary, in each measure. The rhythms in $\frac{2}{4}$, $\frac{4}{4}$ and (as some say) $\frac{6}{8}$ occur in groups of two; the others, in groups of three. Every group in modern music, as in chant, should be rendered either as a rise or fall group, according to the disposition of the melody and the nature of the text. In this way every group before the melodic climax aids the flow to it; and every group after it, the flow to rest from it.

170. Very often conductors will rightly disregard the bar line in the performance of modern music. By so doing they can give greater attention to the musical phrase and its subordinate divisions. In this way a much truer and clearer picture of the rhythmic flow can be drawn.

171. The Gregorian system of rhythm is not incompatible with modern music if its principles are applied correctly. In point of fact, their application will greatly enhance the beauty of modern music. Moreover, in comparing the chant and modern music, the true nature of rhythm can be more clearly explained, more easily understood and more readily accepted by modern musicians.

PART II

CHAPTER XV

GREGORIAN MODES

172. Gregorian melodies are written in definite tonalities called **modes**. A tonality is a musical effect produced by the preference given to the various notes of the scale. It happens that some series of notes reflect joy, others, sorrow; some, gallantry, others, meekness. The choice of notes and the preference given them in a musical selection is called a **tonality**. One tonality differs from the other in that the half-tones are in different relation to the tonic and dominant of the mode. In modern music two scales are used, the major and the minor. The major has for its tonic *do*, for its dominant *sol*; its range extends from *do* to *do* and its half-tones occur from the 3rd to the 4th and from the 7th to the 8th degrees. The minor has *la* for its tonic, *mi* for its dominant; it extends from *la* to *la* and its half-tones occur from the 2nd to the 3rd and from the 5th to the 6th degrees of the scale. Each scale, therefore, encompasses an octave. The major has *do* for its tonic and the fifth above for its dominant; the minor has *la* for its tonic and the fifth above for its dominant. The former, we may say, is built on *do*, the latter on *la*.

173. Two Gregorian modes are built on each of the seven notes of the scale: *do, re, mi, fa, sol, la* and *ti*. This brings the number of modes to fourteen. By changing *ti* to *te* (*ti* flat), however, Mode IX can easily be transposed to Mode I; Mode X to Mode II, etc., as will be explained in paragraph 178. Consequently it is generally said that there are actually only eight modes in the chant. In the discussions which follow, numbers will be used instead of the conventional sol-fa names to simplify and clarify the exposition.

174. Every mode has three elements: a **final**, a **dominant** and a **range**. The **final** is the note on which melodies of that mode end. A melody always falls to rest on the final of the mode. There are (assuming the number of modes to be eight) four finals: 2, 3, 4, 5: 2 is the final of Modes I and II; 3 of Modes III and IV; 4 of Modes V and VI; 5 of Modes VII and VIII.[1] The **dominant** of the mode is the note around which the melody flows. It is, as its name implies, the 'dominating' note of the mode. In the odd-numbered modes (I, III, V and VII) the dominant is always the fifth above the final; in the even-numbered modes (II, IV, VI and VIII) it is the third above the final. The **range** is the octave within which the mode is

---

[1] The finals are set in **bold face** type; the dominants are in parentheses.

MODES ¶ 175-176

written. A melody may not always remain strictly within its range; it may exceed the range either above or below the octave. Gregorian melodies, however, remain for the most part within the octave.

175. Modes are divided into two classes: the *authentic* and the *plagal*. The authentic modes are the original; the plagal are the modes derived from them. The numbers set before the staff designate the number of the mode in which the melody is written. This system is used in the Liber Usualis, the Graduale Romanum and other church music books. **Intr.** 6 signifies that the Introit is in Mode VI; **Offert.** 2 signifies that the Offertory is in Mode II, etc. The odd-numbered modes are authentic; the even-numbered, plagal. The relationship of the two modes consists in this: both have the same final and both are built on the five notes ascending from the final. The authentic completes its range by extending the notes upward to the octave above and the plagal, by extending downward to the octave below. For example, the final of Modes I and II is *re*. The five notes built on the final are common to both modes, the authentic and the plagal. Five notes built on *re* form the common or central fifth of Modes I and II:

The authentic mode (in this specific case, Mode I) is continued upward to the octave of *re*:

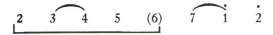

and the plagal (in this specific case, Mode II) is continued downward to the octave of *la*:

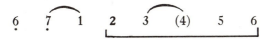

The relation of the two modes and the importance of the central fifth may be seen when both are joined:

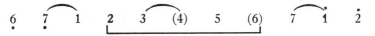

176. Since the dominant of the authentic modes is five notes removed from the final, the melodies of these modes are quite active because of the large space in which they move. On the other hand, the dominant of the plagal modes is only a third from the final; the space is so limited between the final and dominant that plagal melodies are naturally expected to be quite sober and quiet and generally more restful. The authentic modes often delight in intervals of fifths; that is, from the final to the dominant, as *re - la* or *la - re* in Mode I and *sol - re* or *re - sol* in Mode VII.

177. The system of the modes as built according to the principles laid down in paragraph 175 is as follows:

```
Mode                      Central Fifth
                    ┌─────────────────────┐
  I                 2   3   4   5  (6)   7̂   1̇   2̇
 II         6̣  7̣  1̂  2   3  (4)  5   6
III                 3   4̂  5   6  (7)   1̇   2̇   3̇
 IV       7̣  1̂  2   3   4  (5)  6   7
  V                     4   5   6   7̂  (1̇)  2̇   3̇   4̇
 VI           1   2   3̂  4   5  (6)   7̂   1̇
VII                         5   6   7̂  1̇  (2̇)  3̇   4̇   5̇
VIII         2   3̂  4   5   6  (7)   1̇   2̇
 IX                             6̣  7̣  1̂  2  (3)  4   5   6
  X        3̣  4̣  5̣  6̣  7̣ (1̂)  2   3
 XI                                 7̣  1̂  2   3  (4)  5   6   7
XII       4̣  5̣  6̣  7̣  1̂ (2)  3   4
XIII                                1   2   3̂  4  (5)  6   7̂  1̇
XIV        5̣  6̣  7̣  1̂  2  (3)  4   5
```

178. It was found that by a slight change of *ti* to *te*, in Mode I, Mode IX could be changed to Mode I; Mode X to Mode II, etc. Thus the number of modes is reduced from fourteen to eight. The only difference between these two modes is that Mode I has the half-tone between its sixth and seventh degrees, and Mode IX has the half-tone between its fifth and sixth degrees:

```
Mode I:    2   3   4   5  (6)   7̂   1̇   2̇
Mode IX:   6̣   7̣   1̂   2  (3)   4    5    6
```

But by flatting the *ti* of Mode I the succession of intervals becomes exactly that of Mode IX:

```
Mode I:    2   3   4   5  (6)   ♭7̂   1̇   2̇
Mode IX:   6̣   7̣   1̂   2  (3)   4    5    6
```

Similarly Modes X, XI, XII, XIII, XIV become Modes II, III, IV, V and VI respectively. It is apparent then that the half-step in each mode in relation to its final and dominant gives a different tonality:

MODES

Authentic Modes

I	2	3	4	5	(6)	7	1̇	2̇
III	3	4	5	6	(7)	1̇	2̇	3̇
V	4	5	6	7	(1̇)	2̇	3̇	4̇
VII	5	6	7	1̇	(2̇)	3̇	4̇	5̇

Plagal Modes

II	6	7	1	2	3	(4)	5	6
IV	7	1	2	3	4	(5)	6	7
VI	1	2	3	4	5	(6)	7	1̇
VIII	2	3	4	5	6	(7)	1̇	2̇

179. During the course of the centuries when the ear became trained to regard *ti* as the 'leading tone' because of its great affinity to *do* the dominant of Modes III and VIII, instead of remaining *ti*, was changed to *do*. The *ti* is now known as the *ancient dominant*; the *do* as the *modern dominant* of these modes. Furthermore, it is said also that when the dominant of the authentic mode was raised, the dominant of the plagal modes changed accordingly, so that the ancient dominant of Mode IV is *sol* and the modern dominant, *la*. Moreover, some melodies contain such a mixture of dominants that it is at times difficult to determine which is the dominant; often there are disputes among the authorities as to the correct mode of the melody. This, however, is of no great concern since the chief duty of the singer of Gregorian Chant is to sing the notes as written, regardless of the modes to which they are assigned.

180. Many people believe that every mode reflects a certain 'mood' or characteristic according to the sentiments it arouses in the minds of the listeners. Adam of Fulda (c. 1450 - c. 1537) says:

"For every mood the first will be good;
The second so tender to grief;
If anger the third one provoke
Then the fourth will bring the relief.
The fifth will be the mood for the joyous;
The sixth one the pious will prize;
The seventh is pleasing to the youth;
But the last is the mood for the wise."

Johner[1] maintains that Mode I expresses a "happy admixture of strength and firmness"; Mode II "forms melodies that are exceedingly agreeable"; Mode III is "characterized as fiery and stormy because of its wide intervals and leaps"; Mode IV is "persuasive and best fitted to express fervent supplication"; Mode V is "almost inexhaustible in its power of producing ever new and charming, and often enchanting, transformations of the few fundamental forms"; Mode VI is one "that moves to tears but tears rather of sweet joy than of sadness"; Mode VII is "aspiring and cheerful

---
[1] Johner, Dominic Dom. A New School of Gregorian Chant. Ratisbon, Frederick Pustet, 1925.

and with its quick passages is a true figure of the restlessness of youth"; and, finally, Mode VIII "presents in its melody a movement that is calm and stately."

181. No mode, and no melody, can be said to be unreservedly characteristic of a particular mood, for the same melody is sometimes used for occasions of quite opposite sentiment. The joyful *Regina coeli*, the Easter antiphon to the Blessed Mother, and the solemn Requiem Introit are both in Mode VI. Furthermore, the melody of the Gradual for the Requiem Mass (with slight variations) is used also in the four Graduals of the Saturday in Ember Week of Advent, in the Mass for the Vigil of Christmas, in the Mass on Christmas (Midnight Mass), in the *Haec dies* Graduals of Easter Sunday and Easter Week, in the Mass of a Confessor not Bishop, in the Mass for the Saturdays in honor of the Blessed Virgin Mary, in the Masses for the feasts of St. Thomas and St. Barnabas, Apostles, of St. Joachim and St. Jerome, for the XXI Sunday after Pentecost, and also for the Nuptial Mass. It would be difficult to find a characteristic common to all these occasions, which warrants the use of the same melody.

182. In the study of the modes, since the dominant is the note around which the melody flows, it is profitable to learn the tones of the sol-fa scale around the dominant. For example, in Mode I whose dominant is *la*, the notes adjoining the dominant are *sol* and *ti*: *sol la ti*. Singers may find some difficulty in singing *sol la ti* but the pattern *do re mi* is exactly like it, consisting of two whole tones. The tone *sol* is called *do*; the series *do re mi* learned in all of its variations: *do re mi do, do mi re do*, etc. When it is translated to the original *sol la ti*, the *la* should be emphasized since it is the important note. The high *do* is next added, forming the series *sol la ti do* which corresponds to *do re mi fa*. The interval *sol - ti* might cause difficulty but when translated into its parallel *do - mi*, it can be sung easily. Next, high *re* is added: *la ti do re*. The interval *re - la* is important for it is composed of the dominant and the highest note of the mode. The next step would consist in the study of the notes around the final, *re*: *re mi fa sol*. There should be no difficulty here, especially since the series can begin on *do*: *do re mi fa sol*; the notes *re mi fa sol* should be emphasized. Then the two can be joined (*re mi fa sol la ti do re*) and the notes of the entire mode learned. Since *re* is the final and *la* the dominant, the chord *re fa la* is very important. Mode I lingers upon these notes in intervals, as *re fa re, fa la fa, re la re*, etc. For models of this mode, the Kyrie of Masses IV, IX and X can be examined; for the transposed mode, the Kyrie of Mass XI.

183. When two or more modes are learned in the above method, the other modes are learned very easily, for the same notes and intervals recur constantly. Little need be said here about the nature of the intervals. Too much stress should not be laid upon the names of intervals: the fact that *do - mi* is a major third or *re - fa* a minor third means nothing to non-musicians. Music must be practical in order to be understood and appreciated. Theorizing in music produces two evil effects: it makes music unfruitful and distasteful.

MODES ¶ 184-185

184. Typical melodies of the various modes, taken from the Commons of the Masses, are classified below; the melodies of these chants seem to characterize the mode in which they are written.

Mode I	Kyrie X, Sanctus XIV, Agnus XIII
Mode II	Gloria XI, Sanctus XI
Mode III	Kyrie II, Gloria XIV
Mode IV	Kyrie III, Gloria IV, Sanctus III, Agnus V
Mode V	Kyrie VIII, Gloria VIII, Sanctus IX
Mode VI	Sanctus VIII, Agnus VIII
Mode VII	Kyrie VI, Gloria IX
Mode VIII	Kyrie I, Gloria III, Sanctus IV

185. It has already been said (par. 4) that any modern key may be chosen for a Gregorian melody provided the Gregorian intervals are respected. The melody will always be the same if the intervals are retained: the change of key changes only the pitch, not the melody. The Kyrie of the Requiem Mass, for example, may be sung in any key; it is reproduced here in four different keys.

Fig. 112

186. To find a convenient key for any Gregorian melody the following procedure may be used:

(1) Find the highest sol-fa note of the melody; (2) Make that note the highest piano note which the choir can sing with ease;. (3) From that note determine what piano note is *do* of the sol-fa notes. That note will be the key for the Gregorian melody. As a specific example, this procedure can be applied to the Requiem Gradual:

(1) The highest note is *fa*;

(2) The highest note the choir can sing comfortably is E, let us assume; accordingly E is *fa*;

(3) If *fa* is E, then *sol* is F♯, *la* is G♯, *ti* is A♯ and *do* is B. The key to be used, therefore, is the key of B:

Fig. 113

If the key of B is found to be too difficult to play, the entire melody may be lowered a half-tone to B♭ or raised a half-tone to C:

Fig. 114

Another practical scheme is based on the dominant. Since the dominant of the mode is practically the middle of the mode and since the notes A or B♭ are practically the middle notes of the voice, either of these two notes may be chosen for the dominant of the mode to be sung.

MODES ¶ 187

187. The following figure gives a convenient key for each mode.

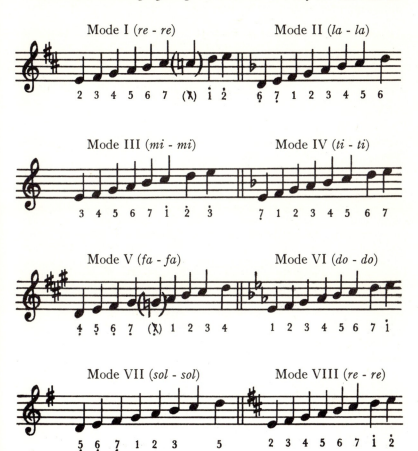

Fig. 115

NOTE: It is superfluous and impractical to include a series of exercises here. Any division taken directly from the chant to be studied can be used as a vocal exercise. It seems more serviceable for the choirmaster to lead his singers in reviewing and repeating more difficult passages practiced as vocalises. In this way the voice is exercised and at the same time the melody is definitely impressed upon the memory of his singers. Thus, for instance, if the melody on the words *et semini ejus* of the Requiem Offertory presents a difficulty (as it usually does), the passage should be repeated again and again on the sol-fa notes. After the melody is memorized in this way, the passage can be sung to the various vowel sounds. When a rhythmic difficulty arises, the notes can be sung in groups until the rhythm is felt. Finally, the notes should be sung to their proper text and proper rhythm. This method appears to be more practical and time-saving than the use of standardized exercises. Of course, at the beginning simpler passages are recommended. No melody more simple than the Requiem *Kyrie* can be found.

CHAPTER XVI

PSALMODY

188. The psalms comprise the major portion of the Vesper service. This beautiful and rich liturgical devotion of the Church has unfortunately been permitted to fall into disuse. The reason may be the same as dealt the death blow to the chant at large: the introduction of melodies too difficult and too florid to be sung by the laity. Parishes were forced to resort to the use of professional singers and consequently forced to bear a heavy financial burden. Since most of the parishes were unable to support such a choir, the Vespers were discontinued, becoming a memory of the past. As an aid and encouragement to the restoration of this service, therefore, this chapter on psalmody is included in this book. Beginners should not be discouraged by the intricacies of psalmody: it is less difficult to sing a service than to explain it. Furthermore, the details explained here should not be committed to memory since the Liber clearly prints the notation, cadences and rhythmic nuances. After a little practice this service can readily be mastered.

189. Vespers are sung in the manner given below. **Off.** refers to the **Officiant; C.** to the **Choir** or **Congregation; Ch.** to the **Chanter**.[1]

I The *Pater* and *Ave* are said silently.
II **Off.** *Deus in adjutorium.* **C.** *Domine, ad adjuvandum.*
    Gloria Patri, Sicut erat and *Alleluia* or *Laus tibi, Domine.*
III The five psalms with their antiphons.
IV **Off.** Chapter (Capitulum). **C.** *Deo gratias.*
V Hymn with proper versicle and response (designated by ℣ and R).
VI Antiphon to Magnificat, Magnificat and repetition of Antiphon.
VII **Off.** *Dominus vobiscum.* **C.** *Et cum spiritu tuo.*
VIII **Off.** Oration of the day. **C.** *Amen.*
IX Commemorations, if any.
X **Off.** *Dominus vobiscum.* **C.** *Et cum spiritu tuo.*
XI **Ch.** *Benedicamus Domino.* **C.** *Deo gratias.*
XII **Off.** *Fidelium animae.* **C.** *Amen.*
XIII *Pater noster* silently.
XIV **Off.** *Dominus det nobis suam pacem.* **C.** *Et vitam aeternam. Amen.*
XV **C.** The proper anthem of the Blessed Mother with versicle and response. **Off.** Oration. **C.** *Amen.*
XVI **Off.** *Divinum auxilium.* **C.** *Amen.*

---

[1] All references given apply to the Liber Usualis, edition No. 801, published by Desclée, Tournai, Belgium.

PSALMODY ¶ 190-194

I

190. The congregation recites the *Pater noster* (Our Father) and *Ave* (Hail Mary) silently with the officiant, after which he intones the *Deus in adjutorium* in either the festal or the solemn tone as given on page 250 of the Liber. The choir replies with the *Domine, ad adjuvandum*, the *Gloria Patria*, and the *Sicut erat*. The *Alleluia* is added on all Sundays during the year except from Septuagesima Sunday to Palm Sunday inclusive. On these days the *Laus tibi, Domine* is substituted.

II

191. The officiant then intones the first antiphon to the asterisk. On all double feasts the antiphons are sung in full before and after each psalm. On semi-double and lesser feasts, however, the antiphon preceding the psalm is sung to the asterisk; after the psalm it is sung in full. On double feasts, therefore, the officiant intones the first antiphon to the asterisk and the choir continues it. On semi-double and lesser feasts, after the officiant has intoned the antiphon to the asterisk, the chanter intones the first verse of the psalm. The first section of the choir joins at the second half and completes the verse; the other half of the choir sings the second verse. The two sections alternate thus up to and including the *Sicut erat*, after which the chanter and both choirs sing the antiphon in full. The ordinary Sundays of the year are semi-double.

192. When the words of the antiphon are identical with the first words of the psalm, they are not repeated but are fused into the psalm. So, for instance, the first words of the first antiphon for ordinary Sundays are *Dixit Dominus* and the first psalm begins *Dixit Dominus Domino meo*. When, therefore, the officiant has intoned the words *Dixit Dominus* of the antiphon, the chanter continues *Domino meo* and the first half of the choir joins him at *Sede a dextris*; the second half then sings the second verse, the first half the third verse, etc.

193. The chanter intones all the other antiphons and the first half of the first verse. The two sections of the choir (or congregation) then alternate throughout the psalm including the *Gloria Patri* and *Sicut erat*. All repeat the antiphon in full after each psalm. The Vespers for Eastertide have but one antiphon (see par. 215).

194. The antiphon to the psalm may be written in any one of the eight modes. The psalm tone, however, always follows the mode of the antiphon. If the psalm tone has more than one final cadence (par. 198), that cadence is chosen which will best join the end of the psalm to the beginning of the antiphon after the last verse. It can readily be concluded from this that the liturgy intends antiphon and psalm to be considered and rendered as a complete entity.

III

195. The first verse of each psalm is composed of: (a) an **intonation**; (b) a **reciting tone**; (c) a **mediant cadence**; (d) a **reciting tone** for the **second** half; (e) a **final cadence.** Longer verses are broken by (f) a **flex**. All other verses of the psalm follow the same pattern except that they do not have an intonation (see pages 112 to 117 of the Liber).

196. The intonation. The intonation forms the connecting link between the last note of the antiphon and the reciting note of the psalm. It is used for the first verse only; all succeeding verses begin with the reciting tone. The intonation occurs on the first syllables of the words regardless of their verbal character. The rhythm of the intonation will follow the nature of the syllable. Example:

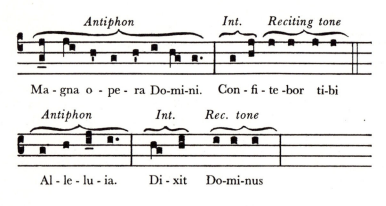

Fig. 116

The intonation consists of one note and a neume in Modes[1] I, III, IV and VI; of three single notes in Modes II, V and VIII; of two neumes in Mode VII.

197. The reciting tone. The reciting tone is the dominant of the mode in which the psalm is written. In Modes III and VIII it is *do*, the modern dominant; in Mode IV it is *la*. It is the same in both parts of the verse except in the *Tonus Peregrinus* which will be considered separately (par. 213). All the verses of the psalms, except the first, begin on the reciting tone.

198. The mediant and final cadences. A cadence is a melodic formula that leads the various parts of a versicle to rest. Each psalm verse is divided into two parts, the first ending in the mediant and the second in the final cadence. All the modes except VI have but one mediant cadence. But all except Modes II, V and VI have more than one final cadence. When a psalm tone is given, its final

---

[1] The Liber refers to the Modes as Tones. In this chapter the terms 'tones' and 'modes' are to be considered synonymous.

cadence is designated by either a small or a capital letter of the alphabet. The use of the small letter indicates that the note represented is not the final of the mode (par. 174). A capital letter signifies that the note on which the cadence ends is also the final of the mode in which the psalm tone is written. The letters used represent the sol-fa notes in this order:

do	re	mi	fa	sol	la	ti
c	d	e	f	g	a	b
	D	E	F	G	A	

In the last chapter (par. 174) it was stated that there are only four finals. These may be represented by the letters **D, E, F** and **G** (in sol-fa notes: *re, mi, fa* and *sol*). But since another scale position is at times used for Mode IV, the letter **A** is included as the final of that mode.

199. If a psalm tone has more than one cadence on a certain note, the tone to be chosen is specified by the addition of a small number beside the letter, as: D^2, a^3.

200. An asterisk added to a letter (as **A*** or **G***) indicates that the final cadence is extended to the note above it. These cadences are quite rare for they are only used in two modes: the **A*** in Mode IV and the **G*** in Mode VIII. The first (**A***) indicates that the cadence ends on *la* (6) and is extended to *ti* (7); the second **G*** indicates that the cadence ends on *sol* (5) and is extended to *la* (6).

201. In designating the psalms to be used for a proper Vespers, the Liber gives: (1) the titles of the psalm (its first words); (2) the tone to be used by a number representing one of the eight modes; (3) the cadence (final) by a small or capital letter of the alphabet; (4) the page on which that psalm is to be found. For example, we may find these designations before the antiphons of proper Vespers:

Psalms: 1. Dixit Dominus. l.g.*p*.128. —2. Confitebor. $3a^2$. *p*.136. —3. Beatus vir. 4.A*. *p*.144. —4. Laudate pueri. 1.a^3. *p*.148. —5. In exitu. 8.G. *p*.159.

This means: The first psalm is the *Dixit Dominus* in Mode (or Tone) I with the cadence on *sol* (which is not the final) as found on page 128. The second psalm is the *Confitebor* in Tone III with the second of the *la* endings as found on page 136. The third psalm is the *Beatus vir* in Tone IV with the ending on *la* which is extended to *ti*. The fourth psalm is the *Laudate pueri* in Tone I with the cadence on the third of the *la* endings as found on page 148. The fifth psalm is the *In exitu* in Tone VIII with the cadence on *sol* which is the final of that Mode as found on page 159.

202. The cadences always center around the last or the last two accented syllables of the verse. Hence there are two kinds of cadences: a cadence of one and a cadence of two accents. A cadence of one accent may be preceded by one, two or three preparatory syllables.

203. The accents affected by the cadence are printed (in the Liber) in **heavy** type: the preparatory syllables are printed in *italics*. It may happen on infrequent occasions that because of a peculiar disposition of the words the cadence will occur on a syllable that is not accented. In a cadence of one accent, for example, provision is made for the extra syllable between the accent and the last syllable in dactylic words (par. 97).

| se - | men | é - | | jus. | spondee |
| no - | men | Dó- | mi - | ni. | dactyl |

Fig. 117

This extra note is printed as an open note in the chant books. In a cadence of two accents, two open notes are supplied for the extra syllables in dactyls:

(a)	i -	ni -	mí-		cos	mé-		os.
(b)			ó-	pe-	ra	Dó-	mi-	ni.
(c)	mi -	se -	rá-		tor	Do-	mi-	nus
(d)			pó-	pu-	lo	sú-		o.

(a) 2 spondees   (c) 1 spondee and 1 dactyl
(b) 2 dactyls   (d) 1 dactyl and 1 spondee

Fig. 118

204. Monosyllabic words that occur within the cadence convert spondees into dactylic cadences (Fig. 119 [a]) and move the place of the cadence in dactyls (Fig. 119 [b]):

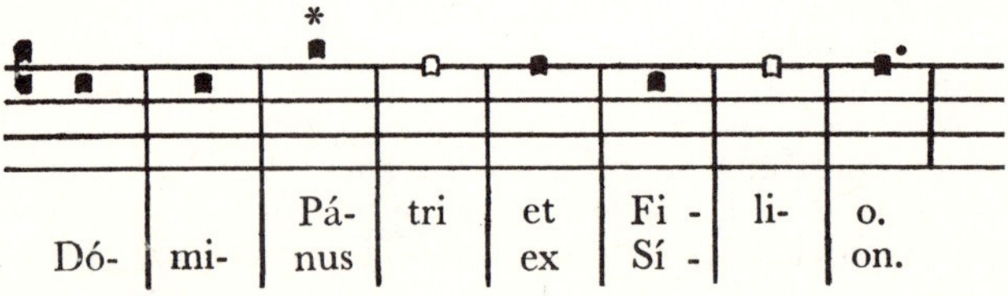

| | | Pá- | tri | et | Fi - | li- | o. |
| Dó- | mi- | nus | | ex | Sí - | | on. |

(a) 1 spondee and 1 monosyllable
(b) 1 dactyl and 1 monosyllable

Fig. 119

PSALMODY

It should be noted that although the last syllable of the word *Dominus* in (b) is affected by the cadence, the syllable itself is not stressed. The melody but not the nature of the last syllable is changed. As a last syllable it must be rendered softly.

205. Provisions are made for two syllables between two accents. If, however, more than two syllables occur between them, the cadence is shifted to another syllable:

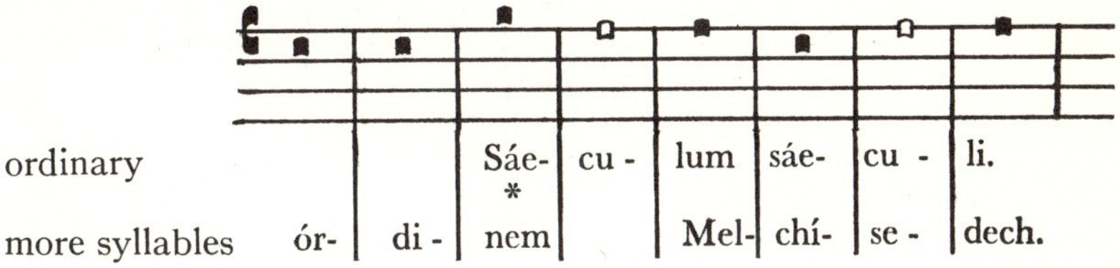

			Sáe-	cu -	lum	sáe-	cu -	li.
ordinary			*					
more syllables	ór-	di -	nem		Mel-	chí-	se -	dech.

Fig. 120

206. Each half of the verse ends in a cadence; the first half closes in the so-called mediant cadence, the second half in the final cadence. Each half possesses its own climax to which the rhythm rises in dynamics and agogics and from which it falls to rest. Since the mediant cadence is the end of only half the verse, it is less retarded than the final cadence. But since the first half is a complete phrase, there must be a definite pause of at least two pulsations before the second half is begun. When sections of choirs alternate, there seems to be no need for a pause between the verses. In order to avoid giving an impression of haste in singing, especially since each beginning is active, it is well for the singers to exaggerate the pause after the mediant cadence. When Vespers are sung in churches with prolonged echoes, the pause between the two halves of the verses might even be extended to three or four pulsations. The pause suggested is important; the lack of all pause will convey the idea of a hurried and rushed service. Activity at the beginning of all verses avoids dragging; a restful pause at the halves prevents rushing. An asterisk appears at the mediant cadence in the text of the verses.

207. **A cadence of one accent** is found in the mediant of Tones II, V and VIII. The accent of a spondee will always occur on a rhythmic rise note and the accent of a dactyl will always occur on a rhythmic fall note. In this way the spondaic accent is always light and brief; the dactylic is always stressed (pars. 106, 107). This rhythmic arrangement is assured by the addition of the open note in dactylic cadences. (see Fig. 117.)

208. **A cadence of two accents** occurs in the mediant of Tones I, III and VII, and in the final of Tones V and VII. Since the first of the accents effected by the cadence is always higher in melody than the second, the first should be considered the climax of the verse. The spondees and dactyls are treated as in the former cadence. Figure 119 presents an example of the arrangement of syllables.

209. A cadence of one accent with one preparatory syllable occurs in the final of Tones II and III (first form) and in the mediant of Tone VI. The syllable before the last accent is affected regardless of its verbal character.

Fig. 121

210. A cadence of one accent and two preparatory syllables occurs in the mediant of Tone IV and in the final of Tones I, III (second form), VI and VIII. The two syllables before the accent are affected by this cadence. The preparatory syllables of tone IV (mediant) and Tones I and VIII (final) consist of two single notes; of Tone III of two neumes, of Tone VI of one note and one neume. The notes or neumes are accorded a rhythm in keeping with the nature of the syllable they adorn.

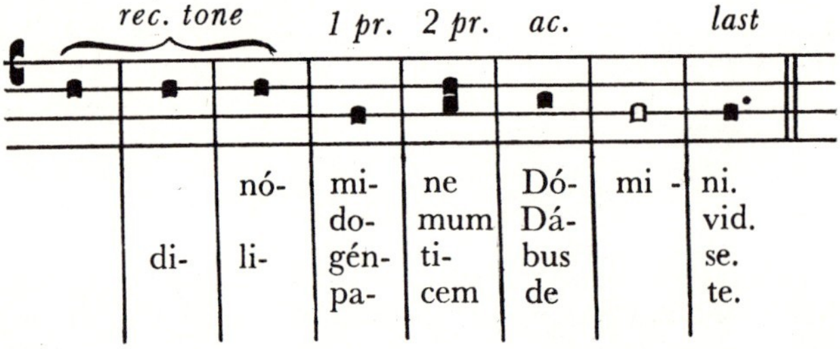

Fig. 122

211. A cadence of one accent and three preparatory syllables occurs in the final of Tone IV. This is perhaps the most intricate of all the cadences not only because of the three preparatory syllables but also because of the special form of the dactylic cadence.

212. The special form of the dactylic cadence is described in the Liber as 'an extra note added in anticipation of the accent in dactylic cadences'. In the accent-cadences as described above, the accents of spondees are always light and those of dactyls always stressed (par. 207). In this special form of cadence, however, the rhythm of the accent is reversed: the accents of spondees are always stressed (because they occur on the neume), and the accents of dactyls are always light (because they occur on the isolated note before the

PSALMODY ¶ 212

neume). This effect is produced by the addition of an open note which is used only on the accents of dactyls. This type of cadence was anticipated in the discussion of the effect of the accent on a rhythmic rise and fall note (par. 105). To master this cadence the singer need only remember that the accent of every spondee is sung to the neume (and is therefore stressed), that the accent of dactyls is sung to the open note (and is therefore light and brief), and that the syllable between the accent and the last in a dactyl is sung to the neume. The Liber places a bracket over the open note and the neume; it prints both the accent and the syllable between it and the last in heavy type. This special form of cadence occurs in the mediant of Tone III, in the final of Tone I (D^2 ending) and IV (E ending).

Tone I (D^2)
1 accent and 2
preparatory syllables

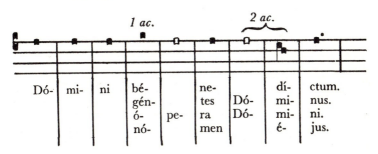

Tone III
2 accents

Fig. 123

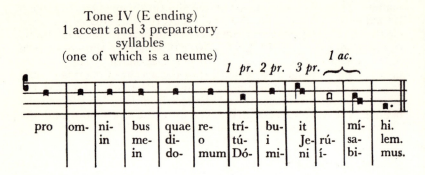

Fig. 123 (cont.)

213. The *Tonus Peregrinus* is a special psalm tone that is used for the psalm *In exitu* which, however, uses other psalm tones too. The psalm *In exitu* is in fact a combination of two psalms, both of which commemorate the return of the children of Israel from captivity. Hence the name *Tonus Peregrinus* or 'Pilgrim Tone'. The intonation consists of a neume (*la - te*) to be used on the first syllable of the first verse only; the reciting tone of the first half is *la*, of the second half, *sol*. Both cadences supply an extra (open) note for the syllable between the accent and the last of the dactyls.

214. Longer verses are broken by a *flex* (Latin for 'bend'). This breaking always occurs within the first half of the verse and is designated by a dagger (†) in the Liber. The flex may descend either a whole tone or a minor third, but never a half tone. If the reciting tone is *do* or *fa*, the flex does not descend a half tone to *ti* or *mi* respectively, but rather a minor third to *la* or *re*. But when the reciting tone is any other note, the flex descends a whole tone. Furthermore, the flex descends on the syllable after the accent: on the last syllable of a spondee and on the last two of a dactyl. For this reason an open note is added for the extra syllable after the accent in dactyls.

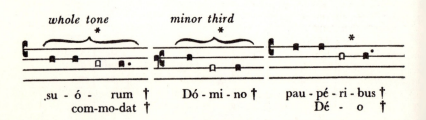

Fig. 124

PSALMODY

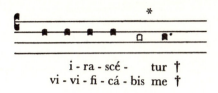

i - ra - scé - tur †
vi - vi - fi - cá - bis me †

Fig. 124 (cont.)

Since the flex is only a breaking or 'bending' of a longer verse, there should be no pause between it and the remaining half of the verse.

215. Vespers for Eastertide differ from the ordinary Sunday Vespers in that the five psalms are sung to one antiphon. The antiphon consists of a three-fold repetition of *Alleluia*. But since on semi-double feasts the antiphon preceding the psalms is sung to the asterisk, one *Alleluia* is sung before the five psalms and the whole antiphon (of three Alleluias) is sung after the psalms. After the officiant intones the antiphon, the chanter intones the first psalm (*Dixit Dominus*) in Tone VII to correspond to the mode of the antiphon. This tone consists of an intonation of two neumes to be sung on the first two syllables of the first verse only. All the other verses of all the psalms begin on the reciting tone. There should be no interruption between the *Sicut erat* of one psalm and the beginning of the next. Each section of the choir sings alternate verses throughout the five psalms. After the last *Sicut erat* the entire choir sings the antiphon in full.

216. Vespers for the four Sundays of Advent have proper antiphons and proper psalm tones to fit them. They are clearly indicated in their proper places after the Mass for these Sundays (see page 323 of the Liber for Vespers for the First Sunday of Advent). After the proper antiphons, the Liber gives the final cadence under the letters **E u o u a e**. These letters represent the vowel sounds of the words *saeculorum. Amen* with which all psalms end. This feature has two practical values: (1) When the psalms are recited from memory (as they generally are in monasteries), the final cadence is given to save the singers the necessity of looking for the cadence under the psalm tone. (2) Since the cadence is printed after the antiphon, the relation of the last notes of the psalm to the first of the antiphon is more readily seen.

IV

217. After the repetition of the last antiphon the officiant sings the Chapter (or Capitulum) according to the tone given on page 123 of the Liber. The reciting tone is *do*, the flex to *la*, a mediant cadence of one accent and two preparatory syllables, a final cadence of one accent. The last syllable is sung to the dotted notes *sol - la*. The choir replies as follows:

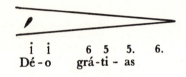

i i   6 5 5. 6.
Dé-o   grá-ti- as

Fig. 125

V

218. The officiant intones the first line of the proper hymn and the choir continues it. For ordinary Sundays of the year the *Lucis Creator optime* is sung in any of the three tones, as given on pages 256 - 259 of the Liber. On other Sundays, the particular hymn is clearly indicated. After the hymn, the chanter sings the proper versicle and the choir answers with the proper response. The versicle and response may be sung in either of two tones as given on page 118. On the greater feasts of the year they have a more ornate tone as given in their proper places; for example, the Vespers for Christmas, Versicle and Response on page 413.

VI

219. After the versicle and response the officiant intones to the asterisk the antiphon to the *Magnificat,* which is always proper. On semi-double feasts the chanter begins the Magnificat after the intonation of the antiphon; on double feasts, however, the choir continues and sings the antiphon in full before the Magnificat.

220. The Magnificat is like a psalm tone. But there are differences. Each tone has two forms, a simple and a solemn, as indicated in the Liber after the antiphon to the Magnificat. The former is used on ordinary Sundays; the latter may be used on principal feasts, that is, on doubles of the first and second classes. Like the psalms, the Magnificat follows the mode of the antiphon. The intonation is repeated at the beginning of each verse of the Magnificat.

VII

221. After the antiphon to the Magnificat is repeated, the officiant sings *Dominus vobiscum*, to which the choir responds with the usual *Et cum spiritu tuo.*

VIII

222. The officiant then sings the oration of the day, which is always proper. The choir replies *Amen.*

IX

223. The necessary **commemorations** to be made may be found in the *Ordo.* They are made as follows. The antiphon to the Magnificat of the feast is sung in full by the choir after being intoned by

PSALMODY

the chanter; the chanter sings the versicle and the choir replies with the response. Both the versicle and the response to the commemorations are sung in the simple form, that is, a descent of a minor third after the last accented syllable, as shown on page 118 of the Liber. The officiant adds the usual conclusion only to the last oration of the commemorations. Other commemorations are made in like manner immediately after the oration, but without the usual conclusion. To the last oration the officiant affixes the conclusion *Per Dominum nostrum* or *Qui vivis et regnas* to which the choir replies *Amen*. If there is no commemoration of a double feast or of an octave, the Suffrage of the Saints is sung on all Sundays of the year except during Advent and Passiontide. During Eastertide, however, the 'Commemoration of the Cross' is used instead of the Suffrage. These are given on pages 260 and 261 of the Liber.

X

224. Then follows the *Dominus vobiscum*, sung by the officiant, to which the choir replies *Et cum spiritu tuo*.

XI

225. The proper *Benedicamus Domino* is sung by the chanter, and the choir replies with the corresponding *Deo gratias* as indicated on pages 124 - 127 of the Liber.

XII

226. The officiant then says, *recto tono*, in a low voice, *Fidelium animae*, etc., as on page 261 of the Liber. The choir replies at the same pitch; *Amen*.

XIII

227. If Compline does not follow, the *Pater* is said silently.

XIV

228. After the *Pater* the officiant adds *Dominus det nobis suam pacem* to which the choir replies *Et vitam aeternam. Amen*. in the same tone as the *Fidelium*, as on page 261 of the Liber.

XV

229. The officiant then intones the anthem to the Blessed Virgin according to the season. These anthems are in two tones: the simple and the solemn. Either may be used at the discretion of the director, according to the ability of the choir or at the request of the pastor. From the first Sunday of Advent to the Second Vespers of the Feast of the Purification (which may occur on a Sunday), the *Alma Redemptoris Mater* is sung (solemn tone, page 273; simple, page 277). During Advent the versicle and response are *Angelus Domini* and

Et concepit, as on page 274. From Christmas to Second Vespers of the Purification the versicle and response are *Post partum* and *Dei Genitrix*, as on page 274. From the Feast of the Purification to Palm Sunday the anthem *Ave Regina coelorum* (solemn tone, page 274; simple, page 278) is sung. The versicle and response are always the same as on page 275. From Easter Sunday to Pentecost the *Regina coeli* (solemn tone, page 275; simple, page 278) is sung. From the feast of the Most Holy Trinity to the first Sunday of Advent the *Salve Regina* (solemn tone, page 276; simple, page 279) is sung. The versicle and responses to all the anthems are sung in the simple form (see page 118 of the Liber).

XVI

230. After the officiant has chanted the proper prayer to the anthem and the choir has answered *Amen*, the officiant says *recto tono* and in a low voice *Divinum auxilium*, etc., to which the choir replies *Amen*, as on page 261 of the Liber. Thus Vespers are concluded. Whatever else is added, such as Benediction, is optional. It may be well occasionally not to add anything to the Vespers, first, because additions are not prescribed in the liturgy; secondly, because nothing else need be added.

231. Not all the psalm tones can be sung to the same modern key. If, for example, the key of C were chosen, the low *la* of Mode II would be the A below middle C, and the high *sol* of Mode VII would be the G above the modern staff. It is suggested therefore that a definite note, either A or B♭ be chosen as the reciting note of all the psalms. Fig. 126 gives the transcription of the first half of the first verse of each psalm for Sunday Vespers, with the note A as the reciting tone for each.

Fig. 126

PSALMODY

Fig. 126 (cont.)

CHAPTER XVII

LATIN PRONUNCIATION

232. The Latin language, like any other language, contains two sounds: vowel and consonant. A vowel sound is produced in such a manner that the air is allowed to pass in a continuous stream over the vocal chords and through the mouth without any obstruction which might cause audible friction. A consonant sound is one that is produced by either a partial or total obstruction of the air passage.

233. There are five vowel sounds in Latin, represented by the letters *u, o, a, e* and *i*. This number should be compared with the eighteen vowel and diphthong sounds in English. The letters which represent the vowel sounds in Latin differ from the English in that each letter designates a single, pure and invariable sound. In English a vowel may have various sounds: for example, the sound of *a* is different in the words *father, all, at, rare*. In Latin, on the other hand, *a* is always *a* in *father*.

234. In the formation of the Latin vowel sounds two organs of the mouth function: the lips and the tongue. The tongue may assume a position low or high, in front or in back. The lips may be fully open, partly open, or closed, either in a rounded or oblong position.

235. The most open of all sounds is the vowel sound *a*. The Latin *a* is pronounced like the *a* in *father, calm, far, garden*. The tongue lies low in the mouth and the lips are fully open. Examples: *al-ma* (ahl-mah), *san-cta* (sahn-ktah), *ad* (ahd), *pax* (pahks).

236. If the tongue is raised slightly at the back of the mouth and if the lips are closed slightly in a rounded or oval position, the sound of the Latin *o* can be produced. This letter represents the vowel sound in the words *saw* or *law*. There is no *u* sound in this vowel as there is in the English *no* (no-oo). Examples: *san-cto* (sahn-ktaw), *a-do-ro* (ah-daw-raw), *bo-no* (baw-naw), *tan-to* (tahn-taw), *ho-san-na* (aw-sahn-nah).

237. If the tongue is again raised at the back and the lips more definitely rounded, the sound of the Latin *u* is produced as the vowel sound in *food* but never as in *foot*. Examples: *tu-am* (too-ahm), *cu-jus* (koo-yoos), *mun-dus* (moon-doos), *so-lus* (saw-loos), *sunt* (soont).

238. If we begin from the vowel sound of *a*, raise the tongue slightly to the front, and close the lips slightly in an oblong position, we can utter the sound of the Latin *e*. This letter represents the

LATIN PRONUNCIATION ¶ 239-243

sound of the vowels in the English words *red, said* or *bed*. It should be remembered that this is a pure sound containing no 'glide-off' to *i* as in innumerable English words: *make, ale, name, lace*, etc. (meh-eek, eh-eel, neh-eem, leh-ees). Examples: *et* (eht), *De-us* (deh-oos, not deh-ee-oos), *se-des* (seh-dehs), *ple-na* (pleh-nah), *Je-sus* (yeh-soos), and also *Ky-ri-e* (kee-ree-eh, not kee-ree-eh-ee).

239. If we raise the tongue farther forward and close the lips in a more oblong position, we can produce the Latin vowel sound of *i* as in the English words *see, be, feed, meet*. *Chris-te* (kree-steh), *i-ni-mi-ci* (ee-nee-mee-chee), *ho-mi-ni-bus* (aw-mee-nee-boos), *no-bis* (naw-bees), *pec-ca-tis* (pehk-kah-tees), *fi-li-i* (fee-lee-ee), *in* (een).

240. Two vowel sounds combined form diphthongs (from the Greek meaning 'double-sound'). Every vowel of a Latin word forms a separate syllable except when the vowels are joined in a diphthong. So, for instance, the *eu* of *Deus* are two separate vowels, each forming a distinct syllable: *De - us*; but the *eu* in *euge* is a double vowel forming only one syllable: *eu-ge*. These two vowels are pronounced in the time value of one syllable in speech but in singing, one vowel must be held and the other inserted quickly. The principal vowel is held and the second is either a 'glide-on' or a 'glide-off' vowel. An example from our own language will elucidate. When the word *old* (aw-oold) is sung, the principal vowel *aw* would be sustained for the length of the note and the secondary *oo* inserted before passing to the next vowel. The *oo* in this case is a glide-off vowel. In the word *new*, however, there are also two vowel sounds, the first being a glide-on and the other the sustained: *neeoo*. Hence before the vowel *oo* is sung, the *ee* is quickly inserted before it. These double vowels occur less frequently in Latin than in English. Very often a *liquescent* (par. 43) is used to facilitate the singing of the extra vowel.

241. There are five diphthongs: *ae, oe, au, eu, ei*. Under certain circumstances the consonants *j*, *y* and *g* representing an *i* sound are added to this number.

242. The diphthongs *ae* and *oe* are pronounced like the simple *e*. Examples: *cae-lo* (cheh-law), *poe-na* (peh-nah), *sae-cu-li* (seh-koo-lee). In the diphthong *au* the first is the sustained or principal vowel, the second the glide-off. If, therefore, a melody of five notes is to be sung to this syllable, the five notes are sung to the *a* and the *u* is inserted before the next syllable. The principal vowel is bold face. Examples: *au-di-vit* (**a**hoo-dee-veet), *Mau-rus* (m**a**hoo-roos).

243. There is a dispute in regard to the correct pronunciation of the Greek diphthong *eu*. Some allow the first, others the second vowel to be the sustained portion of this diphthong: the *u* is the glide-off in the former opinion and the *e* the glide-on in the latter opinion. Still others give it the sound of *oi* as in *toil*. It is recommended, however, that the *u* be accepted as the sustained sound and the *e* as the glide-on sound. Examples: *eu-ge* (eh**oo**-jeh), *seu* (seh**oo**), *eu-cha-ri-sti-a* (eh**oo**-kah-ree-stee-ah).

244. The sound *ei* is a diphthong only in the interjection *hei* which is pronounced *ehee*; otherwise the combination forms separate vowels and syllables. Examples: *re-i* (reh-ee), *De-i-tas* (deh-ee-tahs). These are not diphthongs.

245. The *j*, given the sound of *i* or *y*, forms a diphthong with the vowel which follows it. Examples: *eius* or *ejus* (eh-ee**oo**s, pronounced eh-yoos), *al-le-lu-ia* or *al-le-lu-ja* (ahl-leh-loo-yah), *ma-je-sta-tis* (mah-yehs-tah-tees), *cu-jus* (koo-yoos).

246. The *y* following a vowel forms a diphthong with that vowel. The vowel is always the principal sound of the syllable, the *y* forming a glide-off from it. Examples: *Ray-mun-dus* (**rah**ee-moon-doos). When it appears between two consonants, however, it forms a separate syllable and is pronounced like *i*. Examples: *Ky-ri-e* (kee-ree-eh), *mar-ty-ri-um* (mahr-tee-ree-oom), *cym-ba-lum* (cheem-bah-loom). The Hebrew name of Moses is an exception: the *y* forms a separate syllable although it follows a vowel: *Mo-y-sis* (maw-ee-sees).

247. The *g* when followed by *n* is pronounced like *y*, thus forming a diphthong with the following vowel. Examples: *a-gnus* (ahn-yoos); *si-gni-fer* (see-nyee-fer), *ma-gni-fi-cat* (mah-nyee-fee-kaht). The *g* when followed by *u* and another vowel is also converted into a diphthong sound. Examples: *lan-gue-o* (lahn-g**oo**eh-aw), *san-guis* (sahn-g**oo**ees).

248. The following principles and suggestions for the correct pronunciation of the vowel sounds should be observed:

1. Every Latin vowel is pure; that is, it has but one sound. Care must be taken that English diphthongs do not influence the pronunciation of Latin vowels (pars. 238, 240). In English we customarily close the *o* sound with an *u*—(no as no-oo) and an *e* sound with an *i* (*made* as meh-eed). The last *o* in *Domino* is exactly like the first (daw-mee-naw). The difference between *Dei* and *de* should be clear (deh-ee and deh). The Latin word *meo* has but two vowel sounds: *eh* and *aw*. We English-speaking people would like to insert two alien sounds: *oo* and *ee*, thus pronouncing the word *meh-ee-aw-oo* instead of *meh-aw*. Between the two words *Kyrie* and *eleison* there must be no *ee* sound: kee-ree-eh eh-leh-ee-sawn not kee-ree-eh-ee eh-leh-ee-sawn. Overcoming this difficulty will not only simplify but also beautify the rendition of the chant. It will simplify it, for difficult foreign sounds can not be rendered correctly and smoothly; it will beautify it, for Latin when pronounced purely is very melodious in its wealth of pure and musical sounds.

2. An *i* sound should never be introduced before a *u* unless definitely printed in the word as a *y* or a *j*. *Sae-cu-la* is pronounced *seh-koo-lah*, not *seh-keeoo-la*; *do-cu-men-tum* is pronounced *daw-koo-mehn-toom*, not *dok-keeoo-men-tum*.

LATIN PRONUNCIATION   ¶ 249-255

*3. The succeeding consonant must never interfere with the purity of the vowel. The purity of the *i* must not be disturbed by the *s* that follows it: *no-bis* is pronounced *naw-bees;* *san-ctis* is pronounced *sahn-ktees;* *Chri-stus* is pronounced *kree-stoos.*

249. In Latin there are eighteen consonants: *b, c, d, f, g, h, k, l, m, n, p, q, r, s, t, v, x* and *z.* A consonant is a sound that is produced by an appreciable interference of one or more of the vocal organs with the free flow of air. This contrasts with a vowel sound wherein the flow of air is unimpeded. The organs that can interrupt the flow of air are the tongue, the teeth, the lips or the glottis, or any combination of them.

250. The consonants are generally grouped into two classes: those affected by the continuity of the flow of air; those affected by the use or non-use of the vocal chords producing the sound.

251. Those consonant sounds which totally stop the flow of air and suddenly release it are called *explosives*. The explosives are *p, t, k, b, d* and *g*. The remaining consonant sounds: *f, l, m, n, r, s* and *v* are *sustainable* in the sense that they can be prolonged without the stopping of the flow of air.

252. When consonants are classified as affected by the use or non-use of the vocal chords, they are called *voiced* and *unvoiced*. The voiced consonants, produced with the aid of the vocal chords, are: *b, d, g, v, l, m* and *n*. The unvoiced consonants, produced without the aid of the vocal chords, are: *p, t, c, f, s, x* and *z*.

253. The consonants, therefore, may be classified as follows:

	explosive	sustainable
voiced:	b, d, g	v, l, m, n, r
unvoiced:	p, t, c	f, s, x, z

The voiced sustainable consonants are often sung to liquescent notes (see par. 43).

254. The Latin consonants are generally produced like their English equivalents. There are several notable differences, however, which will be discussed below.

255. The letter *c* is pronounced as *k* or as the *c* in *car* except when followed by the sounds of *e* and *i*. The sounds of *e* and *i* include not only these vowels but also the related semi-vowels like *y* (par. 246) and the diphthongs *ae* and *oe* (par. 242). Before the sounds of *e* and *i*, *c* is pronounced like the *ch* in *chair* or *Charles*. Examples: *ca-ro* (kah-raw), *de-fun-cto-rum* (deh-foon-ktaw-room), *suc-cur-ren-te* (sook koor-rehn-teh), *cul-pa* (kool-pah), *hu-ic* (oo-eek), *lu-ce-at* (loo-cheh-aht), *de-cet* (deh-cheht), *ju-di-ci-um* (yoo-dee-chee-oom), *par-ce* (pahr-cheh), *cae-lum* (cheh-loom), *cae-co* (cheh-kaw), *Cae-ci-li-a* (cheh-chee-lee-ah), *cae-ci-tas* (cheh-chee-tahs), *cir-cum-cin-ge* (cheer-koom-cheèn-jeh), *ci-ca-tri-ces* (chee-kah-tree-chehs), *cym-ba-lum* (cheem-bah-loom), *Cy-prus* (chee-proos).

107

256. The letter *g* is also pronounced in two ways: as the *g* in *girl*, *garden* or *gone* before all sounds except the sounds of *e* and *i*. Before *e* and *i* it is pronounced like the *g* in *gender* or *general*, represented in the phonetic spelling by a *j* as in *jet*. Examples: *glo-ri-a* (glaw-ree-ah), *gra-tis* (grah-tees), *er-go* (ehr-gaw), *re-go* (reh-gaw), *spar-gens* (spahr-jens), *re-sur-get* (reg-soor-jeht), *re-git* (reh-jeet), *gae-sum* (jch-soom), *gi-gan-tes* (jee-gahn-tehs) *gy-ra-tum* (jee-rahr-toom), *co-get* (kaw-jeht).

257. The letter *h* is not pronounced in Latin. Examples: *ho-san-na* (aw-sahn-nah), *ho-sti-as* (aw-stee-ahs), *hic* (eek), *hu-ic* (oo-eek). The combination *ph* is pronounced as an *f*; *phi-lo-so-phi-a* (fee-law-saw-fee-ah), *Phi-lip-pus* (fee-leep-poos). The combination *th* is pronounced *t*: *ca-tholi-cam* (kah-taw-lee-kahm), *Tho-mas* (Taw-mahs). An *h* following a *c* changes the *c* to a *k* sound even if the combination is followed by an *e* or *i* sound: *pul-cher* (pool-kehr).

258. The Latin *j* is pronounced like the *y* in *yes*. Examples: *Je-sus* (yeh-soos), *e-jus* (eh-yoos), *ju-di-co* (yoo-dee-kaw), *ma-jes-tas* (mah-yehs-tahs). For *j* as a vowel sound, see par. 245).

259. The Latin *q* with the letter *u* which always follows, is pronounced like *kw* or like the *qu* in *quick*. Examples: *qui* (kwee), *quo-que* (kwaw-kweh), *qua-lis* (kwah-lees), *se-que-stra* (seh-kweh-strah), *e-quu-le-o* (eh-kwoo-leh-aw).

260. The Latin *r* is never silent or glided over as the *r* in English. It is always pronounced distinctly. Examples: *Rex* (rehks), *ae-ter-nam* (eh-tehr-nahm), *cre-mer* (kreh-mehr) *suc-cur-ren-te* (sook-koor-rehn-teh). Care should be taken, however, to avoid anticipating the *r* when it initiates a syllable. Example: *Ky-ri-e* (kee-ree-eh, not keer-ree-eh).

261. The Latin *z* is pronounced like *ts* as in *cats*. Examples: *zo-na* (tsaw-nah), *zi-za-ni-a* (tsee-tsah-nee-ah).

262. In the combination *cc* before *e* or *i*, the first *c* is converted into a *t* sound and the second, the usual *ch* sound. Otherwise the combination is pronounced as *kk*. Examples: *ec-ce* (eht-cheh), *ac-ci-pi-o* (aht-chee-pee-aw), *ac-ce-dat* (aht-cheh-deht), *ac-cin-ctus* (aht-cheen-ktoos), *suc-cur-ren-te* (sook-koor-rehn-teh).

263. The combination *ch* is always pronounced as *k* (see par. 257). Examples: *Mi-cha-el* (mee-kah-ehl), *arch-an-ge-lo* (ahrk-ahn-jeh-law), *che-ru-bim* (keh-roo-beem).

264. The combination *gn* is pronounced as though it were written *ny*. Examples: *a-gnus* (ah-nyoos), *ma-gni-fi-cat* (mah-nyee-fee-caht), *i-gnis* (ee-nyees), *di-gnae* (dee-nyeh), *be-ni-gne* (beh-nee-nyeh), *co-gno-sco* (kaw-nyaw-skaw).

265. The combination *sc* has the sound of *sh* as in *she* before *e* and *i*; otherwise as *sk* or the *sc* in *scale*. Examples: *su-sci-pe* (soo-shee-peh), *sci-o* (shee-aw), *sce-na* (sheh-nah), *ob-scu-rum* (awb-skoo-room), *scri-ptum* (skree-ptoom), *in-ge-mi-sco* (een-jeh-mee-skaw).

266. The combination *sch* is pronounced like *sk* for the *ch* always retains its *k* sound. Examples: *sche-ma* (skeh-mah), *schi-sma* (skee-smah), *scho-la-ris* (skaw-lah-rees).

267. The combination *ti* before a vowel and following any letter except *s*, *t* or *x*, has the sound of *ts*; otherwise it is pronounced naturally as *ti*. Examples: *noc-ti-um* (nawk-tsee-oom), *gen-ti-um* (jehn-tsee-oom), *lae-ti-ti-a* (leh-tee-tsee-ah), *gra-ti-a* (grah-tsee-ah), *sen-ti-o* (sehn-tsee-aw), *e-ti-am* (eh-tsee-ahm); but *ho-sti-as* (aw-stee-ahs), *ex-sti-ti* (ehks-stee-tee), *at-ti-ne-o* (aht-tee-neh-aw).

268. The difficult word *ex-cel-sis* is simply ehks-shel-sees; *Rex coe-les-tis* is rehkssheh-lehs-tees.

269. Non-Latin words are always pronounced according to the rule of Latin pronunciation. Examples: *A-gi-os* (ah-jee-aws), *Ky-ri-e* (kee-ree-eh), *Sa-ul* (sah-ool), *a-tha-na-tos* (ah-tah-nah-taws), *i-schy-ros* (ee-skee-raws), *Jo-e-lis* (yaw-eh-lees), *cly-pe-os* (klee-peh-aws), *Is-ra-el* (ee-srah-ehl), *Je-ru-sa-lem* (yeh-roo-sah-lehm), *Beth-le-hem* (beht-leh-ehm), *Job* (yawb), *a-do-na-i* (ah-daw-nah-ee), *Jor-da-nis* (yawr-dah-nees), *A-a-ron* (ah-ah-rawn), *Ae-gy-pto* (eh-jee-ptaw), *Mel-chi-se-dech* (mehl-kee-seh-dehk), *Broo-kly-ni-en-sis* (broo-klee-nee-ehn-sees).

270. The following practical conclusions and suggestions for the correct pronunciation will render the singing of the chant more simple, more correct and more beautiful:

(1). Each vowel (except diphthongs) forms a separate syllable in the Latin word. Examples: *con-su-e-tu-di-nis*, *de-al-ba-bor*, *lae-ti-ti-a*, *Mo-y-sis*, *A-a-ron*.

(2). Every syllable should, as much as possible, end in a vowel or at least a singable consonant. Examples: *Ky-ri-e*, *al-le-lu-ia*, *san-ctus*, *cu-jus*, *do-cu-men-tum*.

(3). Consonants must never be anticipated and must never interfer with the purity of the vowel. This purity must be maintained and sustained for every note to be sung on that syllable. Examples: *Ky-ri-e* is sung kee-ree-eh, not keer-ree-eh; *Chri-ste* is sung kree-steh, not kris-teh; *san-ctus* is sung sahn-ktoos, not sank-tus; *pax* is sung pahks, not packs; *om-ni-po-tens* is sung awm-nee-paw-tehns, not awm-nip-po-tehns.

(4). All the notes over a syllable must be sung to the pure vowel sound of that syllable. If there are four notes to be sung over the first syllable of *Ky-ri-e*, the four notes must be sung to the pure vowel sound of *ee*. Care must be taken not to anticipate the *r* and so introduce incorrectly a sound of *eh* before the fourth note. Likewise with the first syllable of *Chri-ste*. The second syllable of *san-ctus* is sung to a pure *oo* sound; the second syllable of *no-bis* to a pure *ee* sound; the third syllable of *Sa-ba-oth* to a pure *aw* sound.

¶ 270 GREGORIAN CHANT

(5). When a syllable begins with a singable consonant, the first note should be introduced on that sound:

Fig. 127

(6). When a syllable ends with a singable consonant, a fraction of the last note should be sung to that consonant (par. 51):

Fig. 128

Much of the charm of the above phrase and similar ones is lost because of an oversight of the nature of the groups. Group 1 is active (ictus on accent, and beginning of word); Groups 2 and 3 are long (dotted notes) and soft (last syllable of word); Group 4 is active (ictus on secondary accent and beginning of new word) and should not be retarded by the two syllables, one on each of the group; Group 5 is retarded somewhat because of its nearness to the end while the ictus is definitely stressed (melodic climax on accent of word); Group 6 is definitely retarded (all ends are long). This phrase has been inserted here as an example because its true beauty is often lost through a misunderstanding of the pronunciation of the words. Every letter of the two words, both consonants and vowels, is singable.

(7). When a syllable begins with a singable consonant, that consonant must be pronounced before the vowel sound of that syllable.

Fig. 129

LATIN PRONUNCIATION ¶ 270

(8). When a phrase ends in a singable consonant, the last note is softly closed on that consonant.

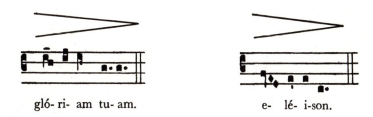

gló- ri- am tu- am.   e- lé- i-son.

Fig. 130

In the above example, as the *ah* of the last syllables of *gloriam* and *tuam* are diminished, the *m* is inserted like a very soft hum. But when the phrase ends in an unsingable consonant, that consonant is pronounced so softly that it is not heard. The reason for the silence lies in the fact that the vowel is closed so softly that the consonant that follows it, even if pronounced, is not heard. If it were heard, the consonant would be louder than the end of the vowel. In other words, the dynamics would open on the consonant after closing on the vowel. This feature has practical value, too, for if two or more members of the choir do not pronounce the consonant exactly together, a double or prolonged sound will be heard. For example, if a final *s* is pronounced at different times by different members, the result is a series of the letter, approximating a hiss.

so-lus sanctus.   vé-ni- et.

Fig. 131

¶ 270 GREGORIAN CHANT

As sung by the Monks of Solesmes, final *s* at the ends of phrases is rarely heard.

(9). The singing of the chant progresses from the vowel sound of one syllable to the vowel sound of the next. The consonants are inserted briskly but smoothly between them.

(10). The vocal organs must never change their position during the singing of a vowel sound. In the Requiem Introit, for instance, the vowel sound of the second syllable of *e-is* (ee) is not to be changed for the eight notes sung to it.

(11). Every syllable is given at least one basic pulsation (par. 47). This time value affords ample opportunity to pronounce every syllable distinctly. Care should, however, be exercised in the correct recitation of dactylic words. The syllable between the accented syllable and the last syllable in a dactylic word has been abbreviated in the course of the centuries in speech (par. 94) but it must not be shortened in the chant. It often happens that this syllable occurs in the cadence of divisions where length is always introduced. If it is shortened, the smooth flow to rest is invariably destroyed and it will seem that the rhythm 'tripped' before it fell to rest. The following illustration gives examples of dactylic words whose syllable between the accented and final syllable is shortened.

mysté-ri- um,   gén-ti- um.

de - féctu - i.

Fig. 132

PART III

CHAPTER XVIII

THE MASS AND THE CHANT

271. The Liturgy can be defined as the mystical Body of Christ living the life of Christ in a mystical way. It is the renewing and reviewing of Christ's life by the Church through the sacred ceremonies. Herein lies the chief difference between a liturgical and a non-liturgical devotion: in the former, the Church acts as a corporate person; in the latter, the individual acts in a personal capacity. A liturgical devotion is a public act; a non-liturgical devotion, private. Essentially, the first is performed by two or more persons acting together according to the rite prescribed by the Church; the other may be performed by one or more persons according to the tastes of the individual.

272. Because the liturgical functions are public, corporate exercises, they must necessarily be performed by at least two persons of whom one places the petitions and conducts the rite and the other approves and consents to the acts. The sacred ceremonies are conducted in the form of a meeting of the faithful under the direction of their spiritual leader, the priest. In the Mass, in which we are at present particularly interested, the priest and the attendants offer the sacrifice together. Under most circumstances, the only participation of the laity with the priest at the altar is through the medium of the voice. This can be done either through the reciting or the singing voice. In the dialogue Mass the medium is recitation or speech; in the sung or High Mass the medium is song. For the former special permission of the Bishop is needed; the latter is prescribed, approved and highly encouraged by the Church.

273. In the course of the centuries when the chant was gradually replaced by figured music, professional singers and trained choirs were introduced into the Church because the laity could no longer participate in such difficult and involved song. Much of this music is not only sanctioned but also encouraged by the Church. But this historic replacement has nevertheless relegated the faithful to the sad position of "silent spectators", as Pius XI calls them. The closest bond that the laity can form with the priest at the altar is its physical presence in church. Beyond this the congregation can do nothing except, perhaps, read their missals silently and privately while the priest celebrates the Mass. For many centuries the Popes have constantly clamored with all the authority of their apostolic office for

a return of the laity to the sacred ceremonies. It was not, however, until the Motu Proprio of Pius X was published that a definite reform was launched.

274. In order that the liturgical nature of the Mass and the people's place in it be understood clearly, the Mass must be considered a public, community devotion. It may readily be compared to a civic meeting: the priest corresponds to the chairman; the people, to the attendants at the meeting. The priest is indeed the duly authorized chairman ordained by the Church to conduct the sacred meeting in Her name and according to Her regulations. The faithful as free citizens of the Church of God, duly incorporated into that Body through the waters of Baptism, have the right to a vote and a voice in the transactions. The House of God, the parish church, is the appointed meeting-hall.

275. The Mass may be divided into five parts: (1) the school; (2) the offertory; (3) the thanksgiving; (4) the banquet; and (5) the dismissal. Each part (except one) begins with the priest's greeting to his people and the people's reply, and ends with the people's assent and approval to what he has done in his and their name.

276. The priest greets his people with the familiar *Dominus vobiscum* to which the people reply, *Et cum spiritu tuo*.[1] The *Dominus vobiscum*, meaning "May the Lord be with you", is similar to our "Good-bye", a contraction of the words "May God be with ye." The people return the greeting in the words *Et cum spiritu tuo*, meaning: "And with thy spirit."

277. The people voice their approval at the end of each part of the Mass with the word *Amen*[2], meaning "May it be so." This corresponds to the modern "aye" used to give consent to the chairman's motion: "All in favor, signify by saying 'aye' ". The *Amen* is, therefore, the liturgical "aye". An ancient writer has said, "All

---

[1] The reply, *Et cum spiritu tuo*, should always be made in a steady, joyful voice expressive of the holy joy and lively faith abiding in the hearts of the faithful. All the syllables are of equal length, except the last. The two syllables *tu*-are so different in nature that they should not sound alike in rendition. The -*tu*, in *spiritu*, as the last syllable of a word, is soft; the *tu*-, of *tuo*, as the first syllable of a new word and also as an accented syllable, is sung rather loudly and briskly. It is also the climax of the entire phrase. There is, then, a gradual crescendo to this syllable and a decrescendo from it. The last syllable, -*o* of *tuo*, is begun softly and is prolonged into silence.

[2] The *Amen*, too, should be rendered in a lively, brisk manner, the first syllable being the beginning of a word and an accented syllable, is brief and rather loud; the second syllable, as the end of a word is long and soft, tapering off into silence. Furthermore, since it is unlawful to accompany the priest's singing with the organ, it is inconsistent to accompany the choir or congregation when it gives the response. It is quite impractical, too, for the organist must often delay the reply until the right key is found. There should be no delay. The *Et cum spiritu tuo* should follow immediately upon the *Dominus vobiscum* not unlike grateful replies which follow heartfelt greetings in our social life. The *Amen*, too, should be intimately joined to the priest's prayer as a lusty "aye" follows a desired resolution. Our meetings in God's House should manifest every sentiment of joy and love. There is no choir or congregation so deficient in the musical art that it cannot sing the simple responses without the aid or distraction of the organ.

reply, 'Amen', which means 'Let it be so as you ask' and 'That which you say is true.' In this simple word is embodied whatever the priest has said in many words and that word can be spoken with such devotion that he who speaks it obtains no less merit than if he had spoken all. For the Lord, our God, does not regard the multiplicity of words so much as the fervor of our devotion."[1]

278. **The School of the Mass.** When the priest arrives at the altar, the choir welcomes him with the singing of the Introit. While this is a song of welcome to their spiritual director, it also sounds the keynote for the celebration of the day. It announces the reason for the gathering on this day. The Introit is composed of an antiphon followed by a verse of a psalm, to which is added the *Gloria Patri.* The antiphon is repeated. Meanwhile the priest is engaged in a private preparation for Mass at the foot of the altar. After the Introit the choir (or better, the congregation) sings the *Kyrie* and *Christe eleison.* These Greek words can be translated: "Lord and Christ, have mercy on us." This nine-fold plea for pardon reminds us of God's infinite mercy and our infinite misery; it thus disposes us for the intimate union which we as sinful creatures are to enter with God, our sinless Creator.

279. Before the "chairman" inaugurates the business of the day, however, he intones the Church's "Star-Spangled Banner," the *Gloria in excelsis Deo.* This corresponds to our national anthem as sung before all civic and social meetings. Because the priest is the chairman of the meeting, he may choose the tone of the hymn. Consequently, it is impolite for the choir to sing any other than that chosen by the priest. The priest, however, may not intone any but a Gregorian *Gloria.*[2]

280. After the *Gloria* the priest faces his people and greets them for the first time. Immediately after the response he states a proposition in the word *Oremus* which can be translated, "Let us ask God for something." The requests are always consistent with the feast. The people approve the priest's prayer in the word, *Amen.*

281. Now follow the lessons of the day in the readings from the Old and the New Testament. In the older masses the so-called epistle was always a selection from the Old Testament. Today, especially on Sundays, selections are chosen from parts of the New Testament other than that of the four gospels. The Gradual follows this instruction. It is a joyful melody expressing thanks for the instruction received.[3]

---

[1] De Ponte, S. J., *De christianis hominis perfectione* (Coloniae: Agrippinae, 1625). Quoted by Gihr, The Holy Sacrifice of the Mass (St. Louis, Mo. :Herder, 1933) p. 425.

[2] There should be some understanding between the priest and the choir as to what Mass he intends to sing. The organist should give the priest the proper key by playing the intonation of the *Gloria* for him. Then the choir will be able to begin at the *Et in terra pax* without hesitation. While this is practical in that it saves time, it is also fitting in that it lends dignity to the celebration.

[3] It was sung in former times on an elevated platform; hence, the name Gradual, meaning 'a step'.

282. The *Alleluia* and its versicle which follows the Gradual is a preparation for the reading of the New Testament selection. In former years a procession was held from the Epistle side of the altar, through the church and back to the Gospel side, during which the versicle was sung alternately with the verses of an appropriate psalm. The Gospel book was carried between two lighted candles at the head of the procession. We still have with us a remnant of this custom in the short procession from the Epistle to the Gospel side of the altar in the solemn Masses. On the Sundays of Lent and on feasts characterized by penance, a Tract takes the place of the *Alleluia*. During the Easter season, there is no Gradual.

283. The portion of the Mass between the Epistle and the Gospel is indeed the musical part of the Mass. The most ornate melodies are sung; the priest performs no rite: he sits and listens. During most of the other selections the priest is attending to prescribed functions but during this part the Church asks him, as it were, to relax and to enjoy Her short musical program.

284. The priest greets his people before the Gospel as well as before the last Gospel of the Mass, although this is not a beginning of a new part. Perhaps the Church wishes to remind us that the New Testament is the era of God's living with us, the fulfillment of the prophecy: "I shall pitch my tent in your midst." (Lev. 26:11). Then again, the *Dominus vobiscum* may be sung to add solemnity to the New Testament reading or to prepare us for the reception of the good tidings. The priest announces the evangelist from whom the day's reading is taken in the words *Sequentia sancti evangelii secundum . . .*, meaning, "Continuation of the holy Gospel according to . . .", to which the people gratefully reply *Gloria tibi, Domine*, "Glory to Thee, Lord." At the conclusion the altar boy, but not the people or the choir, says, *Laus tibi, Christe*. Formerly, however, all said, *Amen*. After the Gospel the priest may give a homily, an explanation of the Gospel just sung, or a sermon on another topic.

285. The priest then intones the *Credo* in Gregorian which the choir ought to continue in Gregorian chant. This is a mere profession of faith which ought not to be sung in a dramatic or theatrical fashion. It is customary in some churches for the priest to sing the Credo with the people. Such a custom is practical for three reasons: (1) The priest is vocally united to his people while the profession is made; (2) The Gregorian melodies are so plain that the difference between reciting them and singing them is small; (3) It dispenses with the rather clumsy rubric of having the people genuflect during the priest's recitation and kneel during the choir's singing of the words *Et incarnatus est*. There is no place for dramatics in a Gregorian Credo. In figured music where the composer delights in dramatizing the simple profession of faith, the basses will sing the words, "Was crucified, died and was buried" and then, with a sudden outburst the sopranos sing the joyful "On the third day He arose." The Popes have constantly condemned with justice features of the theater in church: they desire to preserve the House of God

as it should be kept: a place of holy peace and solemn prayer. The singing of the Credo concludes the school of the Mass. In ancient times the catechumens, those under instruction to become Christians, were dismissed.

286. **The Offertory Service.** The priest faces his people and greets them again at the beginning of the offertory service. Then he sings the word *Oremus*, "Let us pray." The plural "us" is used even though he performs the act silently. Herein is clearly seen the official and public character of the priesthood. At this part of the Mass the priest offers to God the bread and wine which is later changed into the Body and Blood of Christ. He extracts them from all worldly use and makes them the property of God alone. During the Offertory the choir sings the proper Offertory of the Mass. Since the sixteenth century it has been greatly reduced in length. The only Offertory in its original grandeur is that of the Requiem Mass. In former years the Offertory was sung while the people went in procession to the altar to offer their gifts for the sustenance of the priest and the poor. Today the ordinary collection, the people's contribution, is taken up at this time. But before the priest ends this service he asks the people's consent and approval by singing the last words of the last Secret prayer, *Per omnia saecula saeculorum*, to which the people reply with the customary *Amen*.

287. **The Thanksgiving Service.** Again the priest greets the people with the familiar *Dominus vobiscum*. We are now entering the most sublime part of the Mass, for which the priest bids his people "Lift up your hearts" (*Sursum corda*) to which they reply, "We have lifted them to the Lord" (*Habemus ad Dominum*). Then he invites the people to the service now to be performed, singing, "Let us give thanks to the Lord our God" (*Gratias agamus Domino Deo nostro*) to which the people consent and approve, answering, "It is worthy and just" (*Dignum et justum est*). Now follows the Preface in which the priest, speaking to God, proclaims that "it is truly worthy and just, right and helpful for salvation that we always and in all places give thanks to Thee, holy Lord, Father almighty, eternal God." If the Preface is proper for the day or season, the particular reason is expressed why we should especially be thankful at this time. The Preface generally ends with the prayer that God allow us to join the choir of angels and heavenly citizens with and them say without end "Holy, holy, holy, Lord God of Hosts," etc. This is the *Sanctus* of the Mass. We should realize therefore that in singing the *Sanctus* we in this world have joined our voices with those of the Angels and Saints in heaven and with them seek to praise God in this heavenly song.

288. There is a divergence of opinion among authorities as to whether the *Sanctus* should be sung in full before the Consecration. From the standpoint of opposing arguments, some recent declarations of the Holy See state that the *Sanctus* is to be sung to the first *Hosanna in excelsis* before the Consecration and the *Benedictus* after it. This appears, however, to be an answer to the question:

Is it better to sing during the Consecration or to divide the *Sanctus* in two parts, observing silence at the Consecration? The words of a decree issued Nov. 12, 1831 read: "The *Benedictus* should be sung after the Elevation of the Chalice." On May 22, 1894 the Holy See decreed: "No singing is allowed during the Elevation." Of course many of the modern *Sanctus* melodies are so long that they cannot be completed before the Elevation. No Gregorian *Sanctus* is so long that it cannot be completed before this sacred act. A further argument against the singing of the *Sanctus*, in full, before the Consecration can be found in the Liber Usualis, under the title of "Rubrics for the Chant of the Mass", No. VII. It states: "When the Preface is finished, the choir goes on with the *Sanctus*, etc., but exclusive of the *Benedictus qui venit*. Then only is the Elevation of the Blessed Sacrament. Meanwhile the choir is silent and adores with the rest. After the Elevation the choir sings the *Benedictus*."

289. Arguments in favor of the complete *Sanctus* are given as follows: (1) The priest must recite the entire *Sanctus* without interruption. (2) The Liber Usualis in its melody gives no indication of an interruption between the first *Hosanna* and the *Benedictus*. (3) Pius X in his encyclical clearly states: "According to the laws of the Church, the *Sanctus* of the Mass must be finished before the Elevation, wherefore in this point the celebrant must attend to the singers." This last clause apparently means that the celebrant must proceed slowly in order to enable the choir to complete the *Sanctus*. (4) In former times it was expressly prescribed that the priest should sing the *Sanctus* with the people and that he should not begin the Canon until the *Sanctus* is completed. Each course seems to be supported by sufficient arguments. Whether the *Sanctus* is sung in full or in part before the Elevation, a motet in honor of the Blessed Sacrament may be sung in Latin after the Elevation provided it does not unduly delay the priest.

290. The prayers of the thanksgiving service may be found in any missal. It does not lie within the scope of this book to explain them here. Even a cursory study of the prayers, however, will lend much to our devotion and appreciation at Mass.

291. The thanksgiving service ends with the words said silently by the priest, words full of deep and holy meaning: "Through Him and with Him and in Him is to Thee, God the Father Almighty in unity with the Holy Ghost all honor and glory through all ages." These words signify that whatever we do with Christ and in Christ and through Christ during our lives gives honor and glory to God. To receive the people's approval of what has been done in his and their name, the priest sings the last of this prayer in an audible voice: *Per omnia saecula saeculorum*. The people reply *Amen*, agreeing and consenting that it should be so. Thus ends the thanksgiving service.

292. **The Banquet.** Without greeting the people but speaking directly to God in the name of the people, the priest and the people

MASS AND THE CHANT ¶ 293-296

"are bold to say" the Our Father, or in Latin, the *Pater noster*. In this beautiful prayer clothed in plain but devout music the priest asks our Father in heaven for our daily bread. The people affix the ending plea *Sed libera nos a malo*, "but deliver us from evil", to which the priest silently adds *Amen*.

293. Two requests are woven within this part of the Mass—requests that are intimately allied and complementary: pardon and peace. In the prayer immediately following the *Pater noster*, the priest asks God to deliver us from all evils, past, present and future, and to grant us peace in our day. This prayer ends with the words *Per omnia saecula saeculorum* to which the people reply *Amen*. Then the priest recites "The peace of the Lord be always with us," *Pax Domini sit semper vobiscum* to which the people reply *Et cum spiritu tuo*. Again the congregation asks for pardon and peace in the *Agnus Dei*, "Lamb of God who takest away the sins of the world, have mercy on us" and "grant us peace." Sin divides us, grace unites us; where there is unity there must be peace.

294. At the present time the Communion hymn is sung after the priest restores the Blessed Sacrament to the tabernacle. Formerly it was sung while the people received the Bread of Life. Its present form is nothing more than an antiphon which was originally sung alternately with appropriate psalms. It generally embodies the thought of the day's Mass incorporated into a short prayer of thanksgiving. The *Amen* at the end of the Postcommunion Prayer marks the end of the Communion Service.

295. **The Dismissal.** In ordinary meetings the chairman announces the completion of the session with the words: "The meeting is adjourned." In the liturgical parlance the announcement is made in the words *Ite, missa est*, "Go, the Mass is completed", to which the choir responds *Deo gratias*. In less joyful Masses where there is no *Gloria in excelsis* the words *Benedicamus Domino*, "Let us bless the Lord" or in Masses for the Dead, *Requiescant in pace*, "May they rest in peace" are substituted. But before the people disperse the priest gives his blessing and reads the beginning of St. John's gospel, a reading which was and still is attached to many of the Church's blessings. In it we are reminded that we are children of God through the Word that was made flesh and dwelt among us. The Church seems to imply that since we are children of God in Jesus Christ, we should go out to our daily duties and should live that life of whose fullness we have all received.

296. It is often said that a Gregorian Mass is long. It may surprise many to learn that the difference between a low Mass and a Gregorian High Mass should not exceed ten minutes. If an ordinary low Mass is read in twenty-five minutes a High Mass need not exceed thirty-five minutes. In substantiation of this the tabulation below shows relative differences in time between the Easter Mass and the ordinary Mass. The Easter Mass is longer than the usual Mass for it contains a Sequence. The singing of the melodies other than those noted should not detain the priest.

GREGORIAN CHANT

Chant Selection	Time required in singing	Time required in reciting	Difference (delays priest)
Gloria	3 minutes	3/4 minute	2-1/4 minutes
Gradual Alleluia Sequence	5-3/4	3/4	5
Credo	3	1-1/2	1-1/2

Total difference: 8-3/4 minutes

In our busy day there seems to be no time for these few extra moments of worship, although we waste hundreds of such short moments throughout the day without feeling the least concern about our extravagance. A solemn Requiem High Mass sung as it should be with the whole of the Gradual, Tract and *Dies irae* should not extend over thirty-five minutes. Other Masses are no longer even with a Gregorian Gloria and Credo. Ornate or figured or non-Gregorian Gloria or Credo melodies consume the most time at a Mass. When one part is unduly prolonged we sometimes find it necessary to abbreviate another or omit it entirely. On the contrary, devotion should not be sacrificed to haste. If a Mass sung as prescribed should be extended five minutes, the spiritual gratification derived from the praise of Our Lord should more than compensate us for the loss of time.

CHAPTER XIX

THE HISTORY OF CHURCH MUSIC

297. From the earliest ages of man, songs and melodies have been intimately associated with prayers and praises offered to God. Indeed, words alone do not suffice to express the desires of the heart: words are able to reveal the plain thoughts of the mind but when these thoughts are accompanied by deep feelings of the heart, they are expressed in music rather than in plain speech. Furthermore, when people gather together to offer a common service to God, or rather, to honor God as their common Father, their thoughts and sentiments must be expressed through a common and universal medium; and that medium has ever been song, — song which dresses the words in garments worthy of the divine Majesty. It is only within the last few centuries that this garment has been laid aside. Then, while we laid aside the garment, instead of worshipping God as our common Father in plain words, we have ceased to worship Him at all. In consequence we have suffered the loss of the graces of love and fellowship which God gives when two or more are united in His name; with the loss of grace comes the vices of hatred and war.

298. After the Jews were firmly established and solidly united in the Promised Land, Solomon built a Temple wherein God's chosen people could offer a common sacrifice and could sing His praises. This sacrifice consisted of various religious acts accompanied by melodious prayers, for the most part, the singing of the psalms of David. Synagogues were built later in which the Jews gathered to learn the Law and to worship God in prayer and song. In addition to the sacrifices performed at the synagogues, sacrificial acts were performed also in the home where the father of the family was the presiding officer. On all occasions psalms were sung commemorating the rite and praising God for His goodness.

299. Holy Scripture states that our Lord "went every year to Jerusalem at the solemn day of the pasch" and "performed all things according to the Law of the Lord" (Luke 2:41, 39). At these festivities He joined in the singing of the psalms with the others of His race in the praise of His heavenly Father. Even though Holy Scripture tells us but once that Jesus and His disciples "singing a psalm went forth to the Mount of Olives" (Mark 14: 16), nevertheless, our Lord as a frequent visitor to the Synagogue and as a Jew faithful to the tradition of his people, "did join with His disciples in singing the traditional psalms."[1]

---

[1] Nielen, The Earliest Christianity (St. Louis, Mo. :1941).

300. The beautiful canticle that sprang from the heart of the Blessed Mother at her visit to Elizabeth (known in the liturgy as the *Magnificat*), that Zachary sang at the birth of his son St. John the Baptist (known as the *Benedictus*) and that of Simeon as he held the Light of the world in his arms (known as the *Nunc dimittis*) are so like the psalms in structure, content and inspiration that we may rightly conclude that the singers of the New Testament were intimately acquainted with them and held them dear to their hearts.

301. The singing of the psalms accompanied all the religious acts of the Old Testament whether they were performed in the Temple, in the synagogue or in the home. The early Christians, whether converts from Judaism or paganism, carried this practice over to their own churches. The earliest Christians were converted Jews. We know that St. Paul in visiting new cities used the synagogues as meeting places to make contact with the Jews. He too participated in the old ritual of singing the psalms for, to him and his converts, Judaism was but the foreshadow of Christianity. They held firmly to the principle that Christ came not to destroy the law but to fulfill it. Consequently, although many of the Jewish customs were abolished, as for instance the uncleanliness of meats and the observance of the Sabbath, nevertheless many were retained and clothed in the garb of the New Testament. In the Old Testament Christ was honored as the Messiah who is to come; in the New Testament He is honored as the Messiah who has come. For this reason many of the liturgical rites performed by the new converts under Jewish law are still maintained in our liturgy today.

302. The Acts of the Apostles which tells the history of the first years of Christianity gives many an account of the meetings of Christians in which they "day by day persevered with one accord in the Temple, and breaking bread in private homes, took food with joyful simplicity of heart, praising God" (Eph. 5:19). St. Paul urges them to speak to themselves in psalms, and hymns and spiritual canticles, singing and making melody in their hearts to the Lord (cf. Col. 3:16). St. James advises: "Is anyone glad at heart? Let him sing a hymn." (5: 13). St. Peter quoting a psalm says: "My heart is glad and my tongue rejoicest." (Acts 2: 26). Thus it is clear that from the Temple of Solomon, through our Lord and His disciples, the custom of singing "psalms and hymns and spiritual canticles" has come down to us as a worthy, just, right and salutary means of giving praise and thanksgiving to God.

303. The historical development of the chant parts of the Mass lies in the use of psalms in the early days of Christianity. The early Christians withdrew to the underground passages of the Catacombs and there spent many hours, at times whole nights, praising God in psalms and hymns in preparation and thanksgiving for the salutary gifts they received through the sacred mysteries. They sang the psalms antiphonally, that is, each part of an equally divided congregation sang an alternate verse. Later when they were permitted to celebrate the mysteries in public without the threat of

persecution and molestation (313 A.D.), the melodies became more elaborate. A verse of a psalm that was especially suited to the day's festivity was extracted from the psalm and adorned with festive, elaborate melody. The congregation, however, could no longer sing this ornate selection; thus the order of singing changed from what is known as antiphonal to responsorial singing. In this the congregation sang the verses of the psalm while the chanters interposed the decorated refrain or response between the versicles. At this time, too, the *Alleluia* was introduced into the liturgy through the influence of St. Jerome. This was used as a "refrain" or response before and after the versicle song following the Epistle during Eastertide. Its last syllable is fitted out with a *jubilus*, an ornate melody comparable to the Tyrolese yodel which is nothing more than a melodious outburst expressing the superabundant and overflowing joy of the heart.

304. In time the refrain (now known as the Antiphon) which was sung by one or more chanters grew melodically richer. But while the melody was enriched, the text was shortened. The modern Introit, for instance, is nothing more than an antiphon with one verse of the original psalm, followed by the Gloria Patri (called the Doxology) and the repetition of the antiphon. The Gradual, too, has become so ornate that it consists of nothing but the refrain and a verse or versicle of the original psalm. This too formerly had a responsorial character in that the Gradual was repeated after the versicle. The custom of abolishing the repetition, however, was soon sanctioned by the Church. Its repetition today is optional. The only Gradual which still retains most of its former fulness is that in the Mass for the first Sunday of Lent. It consists of a verse of Psalm 90 as the Gradual, a versicle from the same psalm and finally the Tract: the entire psalm except verses 8 - 10. This psalm which is quoted by Satan, as is told in the Gospel, pervades the whole Mass. The words of the Introit, the Gradual and Tract, the Offertory and Communion are extracted from it. The Offertories and Communions with the exception of those of the Requiem Mass have all lost their responsorial character. In Vespers and in fact in all the Hours of the Divine Office, each psalm is preceded and followed by a so-called antiphon. In order to understand the choice of a psalm versicle for a special feast, it is generally necessary to read the whole psalm for the one verse cannot give an adequate concept of its fitness to the feast.

305. The Commons of the Mass (formerly called "Ordinarium Missae"), especially the Kyrie, Gloria and Sanctus, are of very early origin. They appear in the Liturgy of St. Gregory and must have been composed, therefore, before the year 600. The Agnus Dei, however, was added about a century later. The Credo appeared in the Mass about 800 but was later abolished; under Benedict VIII about the year 1020 it was reinstated for special feasts. These chants are comparatively simple in melody and construction because they have always been sung by the congregation.[1]

---

[1] The dates given in the Liber refer to the earliest manuscript in which the melody is found (e.g., X s. means 10th century).

306. It has been shown that in the development of chant the psalms were sung alternately or antiphonally by our Lord and His disciples in the synagogues of Palestine. This custom was carried over into Christianity by the Apostles and the early Christians. The persecutions of the infant Church, however, were not conducive to great development in music. But after the edict of Milan issued by Constantine the Great in 313, the Church was free to sacrifice and to worship God publicly. More elaborate melodies were composed at this time in the various monasteries in the East and later in the West. We must bear in mind that there was limited contact among monasteries at that time: a melody composed in one was never heard or learned outside its birthplace. Moreover, the method of notation was merely a crude memory aid indicating when the melody rose or fell but not indicating the distance of the rise or fall. Since the conventional signs could not indicate the rhythmic peculiarities adequately there was only one way of transferring a melody from one place to another: one person memorized the melody perfectly and then taught it to another who in turn communicated his learning to others.

307. By the time the great music-loving monk was elevated to the papacy under the title of Gregory I (540 - 604), many monasteries were already flourishing in Europe. The sons of St. Patrick in those days took to founding monasteries and writing music with the same natural facility with which they take to politics today. The famous monastery of St. Gall in Switzerland was founded in 613 on the site of the burial place of the Irish monk Cellach, whose name has been latinized to "Gallus." The beautiful *Salve Sancte* Introit of the Blessed Mother Masses, as also the hymn *A solis ortus cardine*, were said to have been written in the fifth century by an Irishman named "Sheil" and the latinized "Sedulius." Even as late as the ninth century we hear of a Notker who was educated with Tuotila by Iso and the Irishman Monegall at the abbey of St. Gall. It seems likely that Irish monks not only composed but through their travels also spread most of the chant as we have it today. It is true that in St. Gregory's time all but twenty-four pieces of Gregorian music had already been composed. Even these twenty-four might have been composed before his time, although it cannot be proved that they existed before the year 600[1]. Whether St. Gregory himself composed melodies is still a matter of dispute. All authorities agree that it is historically certain that he called together the chanters of the various monasteries and had each teach the others the proper melodies, that he compiled the first book of melodies, that he standardized the melodies for use in Rome whence they spread throughout Christendom and finally that he sent chanters to various parts of Europe to teach the melodies. Thus if the authorized and proper music of the Church is known as "Gregorian Chant", we may feel assured that no one other than Pope Gregory is more deserving of the distinction of the name.

---
[1] Cf. Catholic Encyclopedia under "Plain Chant."

HISTORY OF CHURCH MUSIC ¶308–310

308. During the eighth century Charlemagne urged Adrian to send chanters into his empire to teach his subjects the sacred music as sung and taught in Rome. Adrian sent two monks, Petrus and Romanus, to found a school of music at Metz in Germany. Romanus became ill near the monastery of St. Gall and sought refuge and succor from the monks while Petrus continued to his destination. The monks persuaded Romanus to stay with them after his recovery. One of the most famous manuscripts on the chant dates from his time. It contains the melodies written in crude neumatic nuances which are of utmost importance and held in highest esteem by the monks of Solesmes. The symbolic letters, known as "Romanian Signs", depicted the rhythm so clearly that the Solesmes monks found them most helpful in rediscovering the true nature of the rhythm of the chant.

309. The monastery of St. Gall became famous for another contribution to the chant. In the year 870 Blessed Notker Balbulus (the Stammerer) wrote what are now known as Sequences. He adopted syllables and words to the long jubilus in the last syllable of the *Alleluia* and arranged them in poetic form. In time a special Sequence was written for every Sunday and feast-day of the year, but Pope Pius V eliminated all but four. The fifth, the *Stabat Mater* of the Mass of the Seven Dolors, was added later. The Sequences are still sung at Mass after the Epistle in the place of the jubilus. At the same time another monk, Tuotilo (whose Gaelic name was "Tullach"), a class-mate of Blessed Notker, put words to the notes of the Kyrie chants. These are known as Tropes. Perhaps his purpose was merely practical in the sense that it was easier to designate and memorize notes that are distinguished by different syllables. It seems, however, that the Tropes were never intended or used for liturgical purposes. The Masses as printed in the Vatican Edition still retain the name given the Trope, in addition to their special number. Thus, for instance, the Common of the Mass during the Easter season is designated as:

I—Tempore Paschali.
(Lux et origo).

The words *Lux et origo* are the words of the original Trope. The whole was sung: "Lord, Light and Origin of the world, have mercy on us." We still retain the opening words of Tuotilas' Tropes.

310. One of the greatest incentives to the spread of the chant was invented by a companion to St. Bernard, a monk named Guido. He maintained strong views about the chant and thereby incurred the unpopularity of his brother-monks. He was sent or possibly went of his own accord under the duress of petty jealousy from the monastery of St. Maurus near Paris to Pomposa in Italy. The same fate of an ambitious musician met him there. He then went to a monastery near Arezzo and there apparently he found peace. He set himself to the task of placing the neumes on horizontal lines, one known and designated as the 'do-line', the other as the 'fa-line'. He

later added another line between these two and still another below, all of which formed the staff of four lines as we have it today. The fifth line of our modern staff was not added until the seventeenth century. The Pope, John XIX, was elated at this invention for in it he saw the means of perpetuating and propagating the chant melodies without entrusting them to fickle memories. He summoned Guido to Rome to teach his discovery to others. Because of ill health Guido had soon to leave the city. The monks who had formerly brought about his dismissal from their monastery now welcomed his return. But Guido decided upon Arezzo and remained there until his death. It was he who gave the notes of the scale their sol-fa names. He noticed that in the hymn *Ut queant laxis* for the second Vespers for the feast of St. John the Baptist each division began with a successively higher note. The syllables corresponding to the notes were given to the seven notes of the scale in this way:

> UT queant laxis
>
> REsonare fibris
>
> MIra gestorum
>
> FAmuli tuorum,
>
> SOLve polluti
>
> LAbii reatum,
>
> Sancte Joannis.

The French changed *ut* to *do* which was more sonorous to them; *ti* is the European *si* formed from the first letters of the last words *Sancte Joannes*. To avoid confusion of the sol-fa *si* with the alphabetic *C* we changed *si* to *ti*. Guido d'Arezzo had a strong belief that melodies should not exceed the range of their mode by more than one note above or below. He consequently reduced the range of sixty-three Graduals to his own style and taste.

311. Among the slight changes which the chant sustained during this period was the change of the dominants in Modes III and VIII. In the course of the centuries *do* grew so powerful that it relegated *ti* to the servile position of a 'leading tone'. Consequently, in Modes III and VIII which should naturally have (and did formerly have) *ti* as their dominant, the melody shifted adopting *do*. Hence, *do* is known as the 'modern' and *ti* as the 'ancient' dominant of these modes (see par. 179).

312. During the ninth century polyphony was introduced by Hucbald, a Benedictine monk of St. Amand, in what he called the *organum*. He popularized the custom of adding another melody running parallel in fourths or fifths to the *cantus firmus* of the chant melody. So was born our present-day polyphony. Until that time Church music was strictly monophonic. In the following centuries,

HISTORY OF CHURCH MUSIC ¶ 313-314

however, polyphony gained in popularity, at first gently eclipsing its parent and later, when it reached its peak in the sixteenth century, totally overshadowing it. From that time onward the chant sank rapidly into oblivion until the nineteenth century when the monks of Solesmes revived it on the point of its last breath, as it were. The reasons behind the discarding of the chant lay perhaps in the spirit which fostered the Renaissance. During the Dark Ages men were content to live together as children of God. Their parish church and their cathedrals which stand today as unsurpassed monuments of architecture are symphonies in stone. In everything they saw God the Creator and their common Father and they delighted in gathering together and singing praises to His Name. They lived as they prayed and, having prayed together in song, they lived together as brothers and sisters in Christ and children of God. But when the new style of music was introduced, music which the ordinary folk could no longer sing, they lost the consciousness of their common heritage and became individualized.

313. The Great Awakening or Rebirth is hailed by modern Humanists as "a certain period, about fourteen centuries after Christ, to speak roughly, in which humanity awoke, as it were, from slumber, and began to live." It was "the emancipation of the reason for the modern world . . . for the mental condition of the Middle Ages was one of ignorant prostration before the idols of the Church." "During the Middle Ages man lived enveloped in a cowl. He had not seen the beauty of the world or had seen it only to cross himself, and turn aside and tell his beads and pray. Like St. Bernard travelling along the shores of Lake Leman, and noticing neither the azure of the waters nor the luxuriance of the vines, nor the radiance of the mountains with their robe of sun and snow, but bending a thought-burdened forehead over the neck of his mule—even like this monk, humanity had passed, a careful pilgrim, intent on the terrors of sin, death and judgment, along the highways of the world, and had not known that they are sight-worthy, or that life is a blessing. Beauty is a snare, pleasure a sin, the world a fleeting show, man fallen and lost, death the only certainty, judgment inevitable, hell everlasting, heaven hard to win. Ignorance acceptable to God as a proof of faith, submission and abstinence and mortification are the only safe rules of life—these were the fixed ideas of the ascetic medieval church." Thus John Addington Symonds speaks in "The Rise of the Renaissance." Yet this St. Bernard of the simile is none other than the composer of the *Jesu dulcis memoria* a poem in which he expresses a joy unknown to us moderns. In fact, such is his estimate and appraisal of those who built the great cathedrals and monasteries of Europe one of which is the Westminster Abbey in which his king is proud to be crowned amid the splendor of medieval ritual. He says further: "Science was born, and the warfare between scientific positivism and religious metaphysics was declared."

314. Indeed the Renaissance was a re-awakening, man's re-awakening as an individual as the pagans conceived him. It was

also a rebirth in so far as man who had heretofore lived and acted and prayed together with his fellowman as a child of the heavenly Father, awoke to find himself a selfish, independent and self-centered individual who lived for and in and by himself. Such a rebirth not only delivered the blow that eventually shattered Christianity into protesting religions but it even loosened the ties which bound the members of the true religion together. Individual composers began to write melodies in individual style, —melodies for the most part so complex and involved that the layman could no longer partake in the singing. The plain chant was gradually discarded because it was a plain and common music, because it gave no opportunities for individual performances and aggrandizements. Since men could no longer worship God together, they ceased to live together as children of one God.

315. It is not our intention to condemn the Renaissance unreservedly since it brought about much good. Our present purpose, however, is to disclose that one of its effects upon mankind was the destruction of the community spirit. During the Middle Ages so ingrained was the spirit of community that "the pride of authorship was unknown. It was plain that a doctrine belonged not to him who expounded it but to the Church as a whole. To write a book and so make known the truth to one's neighbor was in a sense to practice one of the works of mercy."[1] The same may be said of building churches, or carving statues, of painting pictures or of composing melodies. The artists are still unknown to us because they did not set their individual names to the work they wrought: they produced not for personal honor but for the glory of God and the good of the neighbor.

316. In regard to science, which was born during this age, moreover, Male states: "In the Middle Ages the idea of a thing which man framed for himself was always more real to him than the actual thing itself, and we see why these mystical centuries had no conception of what men now call science. The study of things for their own sake held no meaning for the thoughtful man. How could it be otherwise when the universe was conceived as an utterance of the Word of which every created thing was a single word? The task of the student of nature was to discern the eternal truth that God would have each thing to express, and to find in every creature an adumbration of the great drama of the Fall and the Redemption. Even Roger Bacon, the most scientific spirit of the thirteenth century, after describing the seven coverings of the eye, concluded that by such means God had willed to express in our bodies an image of the seven Gifts of the Spirit."

317. It is true that science is a blessing but it is true also that unless man adopts religion in proportion to the strength he derives from science, he will use his strength to his own destruction. If he grows individually and selfishly, shedding his intimate associations

---

[1] Male, Religious Art in France in the Thirteenth Century (London: Dent. 1913) p. 34.

with his fellow-man, selling his birthright as a child of God for the gains of this world, his follies will lead him to destruction. Science, the glory of the modern age, has grown so strong that it is possible to carry through the air bombs weighing many tons and with them to lay waste in a few minutes towns and cities, churches and cathedrals, abbeys and monasteries, in which people have lived and prayed together in peace and love for centuries before the Great Awakening.

318. Various attempts have been made in the last centuries to restore the chant to its original purity and to restore it to its original place in the liturgy. All attempts failed except that made by the monks of Solesmes which God in His goodness brought about in the following manner.

319. As a youth Prosper Guéranger, an inhabitant of Sablé in France, took walks to the nearby town of Solesmes and meditated among the ruins of an ancient Benedictine monastery. His vivid imagination reviewed for him the life of work and prayer that was formerly carried on within the walls of the monastery. Prosper Guéranger was ordained in 1827 at the age of 22. In 1831 the ruins of the abbey were put to sale. The following year Pere Gueranger with the aid of private donations purchased it. In the next year five priests entered the restored priory and began the life according to the rule of St. Benedict.

320. It was Dom Guéranger's purpose, perhaps even from childhood, to restore the Benedictine life to his native France. He longed to work, pray and sing as the monks of old did before him. His greatest and most famous task, therefore, was to learn how the monks themselves in the Middle Ages sang the chant. He sent his monks to every monastery in Europe to get a photographic copy of every manuscript that they could find. The result is the famous "Paleographie" library in the monastery of Solesmes consisting of photographs of every page of 365 manuscripts. These were studied, compared and analyzed; from the conclusions principles were formed on which the monks built their theory of rhythm. During the few years since the re-establishment of the monastery the French Government expelled the monks no less than four times: in 1880, 1882, 1883 and finally in 1903 when they were compelled to leave the country. They took refuge on the Isle of Wight near England and there continued their researches. They have since returned to the Abbey but are living in their own property as tenants to a pious landlord who had bought the property from the Government (to whom it did not belong) and had invited the monks to return.

321. Two Solesmes monks must be mentioned in order to make our story complete: Dom Pothier and Dom Mocquereau. Dom Pothier was choirmaster at Solesmes in 1904 when Pope Pius X, a year after his famous Motu Proprio, asked him to come to Rome to head a Commission for the Preparation of the Vatican Editions. While at Solesmes he laid the foundation for his successor as choir-

master, Dom Mocquereau. He built upon the work left by Dom Pothier and after careful scientific research of over twenty years published his "Le Nombre Musical Gregorien" which is and shall perhaps always remain the *Summa* on Gregorian Chant.

Summary

During the Golden Age of the Jewish nation David composed psalms and Solomon, his son, built a fitting Temple wherein the people could gather and sing God's praises. Christ and His Apostles carried this custom over to Christianity where it prevailed until the Renaissance. At the official abolition of the sacrifice of the Passover of the Old Law and the official institution of the sacrifice of the Mass of the New Law Christ prayed: "That all may be one as Thou, Father, art in Me and I in Thee . . . that all may be perfected into one, that the world may know that Thou has sent Me and that Thou hast loved them, even as Thou hast loved Me." (Joh. 17:22, 23). But the world has become less one since it ceased to worship God as one. While the world prayed together, it lived together; since it ceased to pray in common, it ceased also to live in common. It is reasonable, therefore, that the Church, the champion of peace and love, has so jealously kept its medium of expression, its sacred music, and that it rejoiced so jubilantly at its recent restoration.

CHAPTER XX

CHURCH MUSIC LEGISLATION

322. This chapter presents the laws, regulations and intentions of the Church in regard to sacred music. The entire chapter will contain only quotations taken from the encyclicals and pastoral letters issued by the Holy Father to the whole Church or by Ordinaries of dioceses to their respective priests. It is true that only the encyclicals issued by the Holy Father are binding upon the whole Church. The letters of the Holy Father and the Ordinaries, however, while obliging only those to whom they are addressed, nevertheless give us an insight into the intentions of the Church and often clarify and explain subject matter referred to in general terms in the encyclicals.

323. Each quotation is followed by a capital letter which identifies the document from which it was extracted. Those bearing the letters A and B are from the encyclicals of Pope Pius X and Pius XI respectively. They are binding upon the whole Church; the others have an instructive value for us. The letters and their references are as follows:

A: Motu Proprio of Pius X, issued November 22, 1903.

B: Apostolic Constitution of Pius XI, issued December 20, 1928.

C: Letter of Pius X to Cardinal Respighi as Vicar of Rome, December 8, 1903.

D: Regulations for Sacred Music issued in Rome by the Cardinal Vicar, February 2, 1912.

E: Letter of Pius X to Archbishop Dubois, as Archbishop of Bourges, July 10, 1912.

F: Pastoral letter of Cardinal Dubois, Archbishop of Paris, October 9, 1921.

G: Letter of Pius XI to Cardinal Dubois, as Archbishop of Paris, April 10, 1924.

H: Letter of Pius XI to Cardinal Dubois, Archbishop of Paris, November 30, 1928.

I—Need for Reform

324. "Since the Church has received from Christ her founder the office of guarding the sanctity of divine worship, She is certainly bound to direct what concerns rites and ceremonies, formulas, prayers and singing in order to regulate better the august and perfect service of the Liturgy so-called since this is preeminently the sacred action." (B)

325. "It is of great importance that whatever is done to enhance and adorn the Liturgy should be controlled by the laws and precepts of the Church, so that the arts may serve divine worship as most noble ministers. ***And this has been effected especially in sacred music; for wherever these regulations have been diligently carried out, there the ancient beauty of an exquisite art has begun to revive and a religious spirit to flourish and prosper, and there also the faithful, imbued more deeply with a sense of the Liturgy, have found the habit of partaking more zealously in the Eucharistic rite, in singing the psalms and in the public prayers." (B)

326. "Nothing should be allowed in the sacred building that could disturb or lessen the beauty and devotion of the faithful, nothing that could be a reasonable motive for displeasure or scandal, nothing especially that could offend against the dignity and holiness of the sacred rites, and that would therefore, be unworthy of the house of prayer or of the majesty of God." (A)

327. "There certainly is a constant tendency in sacred music to neglect the right principles of an art used in the service of the Liturgy, principles expressed very clearly in the laws of the Church, in the decrees of general and provincial councils, and in the repeated comments of the Sacred Congregations and of the Supreme Pontiffs Our Predecessors." (A)

328. "We think it Our duty to lift up Our voice without delay in order to reprove and condemn everything in the music of divine worship that does not conform with the right principles so often expressed." (A)

329. "Wherefore in order that no one in the future may bring forward as an excuse that he does not rightly know his duty, in order that all possible uncertainty concerning the laws already made may be removed We consider it advisable **to sum up** briefly the principles that govern the sacred music of liturgical service and to re-present the chief laws of the Church against faults in this matter. And, therefore, We publish this Our instruction *motu proprio et certa scientia* and We desire with all the authority of Our apostolic Office that it have the force of law as a canonical code concerning sacred music and We impose upon all by Our signature the duty of most exact obedience to it." (A)

330. "Sacred music, as an integral part of the liturgy, belongs to the general object of the liturgy, namely, the glory of God and the sanctification and edification of the faithful. It helps to enhance the

beauty and splendor of the ceremonies and since its chief duty is to clothe the liturgical text which is presented to the understanding of the faithful, with fitting melody, its object is to render that text more efficacious, so that the faithful may thereby be more aroused to devotion and better disposed to gather the fruits of grace which flow from the celebration of the sacred mysteries." (A)

331. "At first the novelty will surprise some; very likely some choirmasters or directors will not be quite prepared for it, but little by little things will right themselves and everyone will find in the perfect correspondence of the music to liturgical laws and to the proper character of the chanting of psalms a beauty and a rightness which they have never felt before." (C)

332. "By putting the matter off the difficulty would not become less, it would become greater: since the thing has to be done, let it be done at once and firmly." (C)

333. "To achieve our purpose, positive, vigorous and enlightened action on the part of both secular and regular clergy is absolutely necessary." (D)

II—Qualities of Church Music

334. "Sacred music must eminently possess the qualities that belong to liturgical rites especially holiness and beauty from which its every characteristic, universality, will follow spontaneously. It must be holy and therefore free from all that is secular, both in itself and in the method it is performed. It must be an art since in no other way can it have that effect on the mind of those who hear it which the Church intends of music in her liturgy. It must be universal in this sense that although each country may use whatever special forms may belong to its national style in its ecclesiastical music, these forms must be subject to the proper nature of sacred music as never to produce a bad impression on the mind of any stranger." (A)

335. "To achieve its purpose, which is to enhance the solemnity of the offices and help to sanctify souls, this chant must be **sacred,** differing from profane tunes in inspiration, general character and method of execution. It must be **grave** like all that concerns divine worship, inducing recollection, closing the eyes, so to speak, to outward things and opening the heart to supernatural influences; it must be **impressive,** giving the soul a voice in which to utter its praise and prayer and adoration, and echoing that interior world which is in each one of us, and in which religious feeling vibrates so keenly at all times; it must be **catholic,** that is acceptable to all men of all races in all countries in every age, and finally it must be **simple,** with a simplicity which does not by any means exclude art, since a clear pure melody often expresses more beauty than the most learned and intricate musical compositions." (F)

III—The Dignity of the Chant

336. "These qualities (holiness, beauty and universality) are perfectly found in Gregorian chant which is therefore the proper music of the Roman Church, the only music (a) which She inherited from the ancient Fathers; (b) which She has jealously kept for many centuries in her liturgical books; (c) which She offers to the faithful as Her own music; (d) which She insists on being used exclusively in some parts of her liturgy, and (e) which, finally, has been so happily restored to its original perfection and purity by recent study." (A)

337. "Plain chant has always been hailed as the highest model of Church music and We may with good reason set down as a general rule that the more a musical composition for use in church is like plain chant in its movement, its inspiration and its feeling, so much more is it right and liturgical, and the more it differs from this highest model so much the less is it worthy of the House of God." (A)

338. "This ancient Gregorian chant should therefore be extensively restored in divine services and it should be understood that a service in church loses nothing of its solemnity when it is accompanied by no other music than plain chant." (A)

339. "Each part of the Mass and Office must keep even in its musical setting that form and character which it has from tradition and which is very well expressed in Gregorian chant." (A)

340. "Is there indeed anything which exhales the fragrance of Christian beauty and fosters the Christian spirit like Gregorian chant?" (H)

IV—Other Kinds of Music for Use in Church

1. Classical Music.

341. "The music of the classical school also possesses in a high degree the qualities described above, (holiness, beauty and universality) especially in that of the Roman School which reached its highest perfection in the sixteenth century under Pierluigi da Palestrina and which continued to produce excellent liturgical compositions. The music of this school agrees very well with the highest model of all sacred music, namely, plain chant, and it therefore deserves to be used in the more solemn offices of the Church as, for instance, in those of the Papal Chapel. It should also be largely restored especially in the greater basilicas, in cathedrals, and in seminaries and in other institutions and where the necessary means of performing it are not wanting." (A)

342. "We wish here also to recommend the formation of those *capellae musicorum* or choirs which in course of time have come to be substituted for the ancient scholae and established in basilicas and larger churches especially to execute polyphonic music. In regard to this last point, sacred polyphony ought to be given a place only second to Gregorian chant itself, and on this account we earnestly

desire that choirs such as flourished from the fourteenth to the sixteenth century be renewed and revived today, especially in those places where the frequency and scope of divine worship demand a larger number of singers and more skill in the selection of them." (B)

2. Modern Music.

343. "More modern music may also be allowed in churches since good, serious and dignified compositions worthy of liturgical use have been produced. But since modern music has become a secular art, greater care must be taken when admitting it that nothing profane is allowed, nothing that is mindful of the theatre, nothing that is based on the form of a secular composition." (A)

344. "But we cannot refrain from lamenting that, just as formerly, in the case of styles of music rightly prohibited by the Church, so today again there is danger lest a profane spirit should invade the House of God through new-fangled musical styles, which, should they get a real foothold the Church would be bound to condemn." (B)

V—Means of Reform
1. General.

345. "We desire all choirmasters, singers and clerics, all superiors of seminaries, ecclesiastical institutions and religious communities, all parish priests and rectors of churches, all canons of collegiate and cathedral churches and, most especially, the ordinaries of all dioceses, zealously to support these wise reforms which long were desired and unanimously hoped for in order that no injury be done to the authority of the Church which has already often proposed them and now insists on them once more." (A)

346. "All higher schools of church music should be maintained in every way where they already exist and as far as possible new ones founded." (A)

347. "It is most important that the Church should Herself provide instruction for her own choirmasters, organists and singers, so that she may inspire them with the right principles of this sacred art." (A)

348. "So that no one henceforth may seek easy excuses to consider himself exempt from the duty of obeying the laws of the Church, let all orders of canonical persons and religious communities discuss these matters at regular meetings; and just as formerly there was a cantor or director of the choir, so in future in choirs of canons and religious let some trained person be selected, not only to see that the laws of the liturgy and chant are put into practice, but also to correct the faults of individuals or of the whole choir. In this connection it must not be overlooked that according to the ancient and constant discipline of the Church, and in accordance with the cap-

itular constitutions themselves, which are still in force, all who are bound to the choir office should be duly versed in Gregorian chant. And the chant to be used in all churches and all orders is that which, faithfully restored according to the old manuscripts has already been published by the Church in the authentic and standard Vatican Edition." (B)

2. Bishops.

349. "The bishop should appoint in each diocese a special commission of persons who are really competent in the matter, to whom they will entrust the duty of watching over the music performed in the churches in whatever way may seem most advisable. The commission will insist that the music is not only good in itself but also proportionate to the capacity of the singers so that they may always be well executed." (A)

3. Rectors of Seminaries.

350. "In ecclesiastical seminaries and institutions the traditional Gregorian chant must be studied with all diligence and love according to the law of the Council of Trent; and superiors should be generous in their appreciation and encouragement of this matter with their students." (A)

351. "In the usual lectures on liturgy, moral theology and canon law, which are given to the students of theology, matters regarding principles and laws of sacred music must also be duly explained and means should be sought to complete this teaching with some special instruction on the aesthetics of sacred art so that the clerics may not leave the seminary without having right ideas on these subjects which are also a part of ecclesiastical knowledge." (A)

352. "Those aspiring to the priesthood, not only in seminaries but also in religious houses, should be trained from their earliest years in Gregorian chant and sacred music because in childhood they learn more easily what belongs to melody, modulations and intervals, and any faults of voice can then be more readily eradicated, or at least corrected, whereas in later years they become irremediable." (B)

353. "In seminaries and other houses of studies there should therefore be for the due training of the clergy, brief but almost daily practice of Gregorian chant and sacred music. If this be carried out in the spirit of the liturgy, it will prove a solace rather than a burden to the minds of the pupils after the study of more exacting subjects." (B)

354. "But under no pretext whatsoever should less than two hours a week be devoted to the serious and practical study of sacred music, preferably the chant, and this in all institutions and for every pupil; these two hours are not to include the time needed for choir practice." (C)

355. "It is the express wish of His Holiness that in all institutions of ecclesiastical education—even those of regulars—great importance should be attached to the study of liturgical chant and sacred music as subjects of the greatest interest to the clergy." (C)

356. "It is particularly important that Church students and young religious, should receive, in the course of their training in the Seminaries, Ecclesiastical Colleges and Religious Houses, a sound and thorough grounding in the liturgical chant and sacred music." (C)

4. Other Rectors.

357. "Those who are in charge of and take part in the public services in basilicas, cathedrals, collegiate churches and conventional religious houses, shall make every endeavor to have the choir office duly restored and carried out according to the regulations of the Church; nor does this simply mean what is implied in the precept of reciting the office *digne, attente et devote*, but also what pertains to the art of singing." (B)

5. Pastors.

358. "Care should be taken to restore, at least in connection with the more important churches, the ancient choir schools which have already been introduced with very good results in many places. Indeed it would not be difficult for zealous priests to establish such schools even in small parishes and in the country, and they would form an easy means of gathering together children and adults to their profit and to the edification of all the parish." (A)

359. "The superiors of churches and chapels, as also the Prefects of music in the chapters, must be well acquainted with the ecclesiastical legislation relative to sacred music, and acquaint the choirmasters, organists and choristers with them, imposing and enforcing their obedience. It is they who, with the choirmaster, are to be held directly responsible for any transactions in the matter of music to be deplored in their churches." (D)

360. "They are to see that the pieces selected are suitably rendered by a sufficient number of choristers capable of a performance worthy of art and liturgy; and this is why the singers ought to meet periodically for as many practices as may be deemed necessary. To insure this, however, both choirmasters and choristers must be properly paid. In the annual budget of each church a definite sum should be allocated to this purpose, and the expenses of showy feasts must be cut down so as to meet this end." (D)

361. "In the courses of parochial instruction, or on other suitable occasions, they must expound the Holy Father's lofty purpose in reforming sacred music and invite the faithful to second their endeavors chiefly by taking an active part in the sacred functions,

singing in the common of the Mass (Kyrie, Gloria, etc.) as well as the psalms, the well-known liturgical hymns and the hymns in the vulgar tongue." (D)

362. "To this end parish priests, rectors and superiors, especially in the larger churches, should apply all their zeal; availing themselves of the help of some competent person to found their particular *Schola cantorum.*" (D)

363. "The efforts of both secular and regular clergy, under leadership of their Bishops and Ordinaries, either working directly or through others especially trained for the task, should be devoted to the instruction of their people in liturgical music, since this is so closely connected with Christian doctrine. This will best be accomplished by teaching Gregorian chant in the schools, pious sodalities and other liturgical associations. Moreover the communities of religious, whether men or women, should be eager to bring about this end in the educational institutions which have been entrusted to them." (B)

6. Choirmasters.

364. "Since not only the rendering of the Gregorian chant, but also that of certain ancient and modern compositions is left entirely to the choir, there is a danger lest, both in the choice of pieces and the manner of singing them, the ecclesiastical regulations may be infringed. It is therefore necessary to make sure that all the members of the choir are technically competent and willing to observe each and every ecclesiastical regulation, and work for the application of the Pope's *Motu proprio.*" (D)

365. "Every *Schola cantorum* or choir should have its own special musical library for the ordinary performances in the Church, and they must possess first of all a sufficient number of Gregorian books in the Vatican Edition." (D)

366. "Organists must take care in the accompaniment not to drown the voices by constant over-strong registration and by abuse of the reed-stops particularly; discretion is to be essentially observed in accompanying Gregorian chant. Even for the interludes and voluntaries they are to make use of approved written compositions." (D)

7. Participation of the Faithful.

367. "In order that the faithful may take a more active part in divine worship, let that portion of the chant which pertains to the Gregorian be restored to popular use. It is very necessary that the faithful taking part in sacred ceremonies should not do so as mere outsiders or mute spectators, but as worshippers thoroughly imbued with the beauty of the liturgy—and this even on occasions when processions and great functions are being held with clergy and sodalities present—so that they may sing alternately with the priest and the scholae, according to the prescribed rule. In this event we should

CHURCH MUSIC LEGISLATION ¶ 368–375

not find the people making only a murmur or even no response at all to the public prayers of the liturgy, either in Latin or in the vernacular." (B)

368. "It is a part of the authentic ecclesiastical tradition of the chant and sacred music that the entire assemblage of the faithful should take part in liturgical offices by means of this chant; following those portions of the text which are entrusted to the choir, while a special schola cantorum alternates with the congregation in rendering the other parts of the text of the more complex melodies specially reserved for them." (D)

369. "The grandeur of the sacred ceremonies increases in proportion to the numbers who join in them by singing." (G)

370. "The faithful foregather at sacred shrines that they may draw piety thence, from its chief source, through actually participating in the venerable mysteries and solemn public prayers of the Church." (B)

8. Singers.

371. "All liturgical singing other than that of the celebrant and sacred ministers at the altar belongs properly to a choir of clerics. Hence singers in church, if they are laymen, are substitutes for the ecclesiastical choir." (A)

372. "Only men of known piety and integrity who, by their modest and reverent behavior during the service, show themselves worthy of the sacred duty they perform, may be allowed to sing in the choir." (A)

373. "*Scholae puerorum* (junior choir schools for boys) should be encouraged not only in cathedrals and large churches but also in the smaller parish churches. The boys should be trained by the choirmaster so that, according to the old custom of the Church, they may join in singing in the choir with the men, especially when, as in polyphonic music, they are employed for the treble part which used to be called the *cantus*. (D)

374. "Singers in church have a real liturgical office to perform and women being incapable of such an office, cannot be admitted to the choir. If high voices are needed, boys may be admitted according to the ages and custom of the church." (A)

375. "Women may not sing in the liturgical functions unless amongst the people or representing them; they are therefore forbidden to sing in tribunes or cantorias either alone, or more particularly as forming part of a choir. But religious living in community, and their pupils with them, may sing during the sacred functions in their own churches or oratories, in conformity with the decrees of the Sacred Congregation of Bishops and Regulars. At the same time they are absolutely forbidden to sing solos, and we desire that the preference should be given in singing Mass and Vespers, to Gregorian melodies rendered as far as possible by the whole community." (D)

376. "Solos, while not entirely excluded, should never absorb the greater part of the liturgical text. They must rather be points of musical emphasis and accents bound up closely with the rest of the composition which should always remain strictly choral." (A)

377. "The solo voice should never entirely dominate a sacred musical composition. It must only bear the character of a simple passage or melodic outline, strictly connected with the rest of the composition." (D)

VI. Text

378. "The language of the Roman Church is Latin. It is therefore forbidden to sing anything in the vulgar tongue during solemn liturgical functions and much more is it forbidden to sing in the vulgar tongue the parts, either proper or common, of the Mass and of the Office." (A)

379. "It is unlawful to change the words or their order, or to substitute another text or to omit entirely or in part except in the cases in which the rubrics allow the organ to replace certain verses which must then be recited in choir. Needless repetition is also forbidden." (A)

380. "The perfection of Gregorian chant is closely bound up with the correct pronunciation of the words. Doubtless the melody is of itself independent of the text, yet they form but one thing in execution. We may go further: the pronunciation of Latin words has exerted an active and often decisive influence on the formation of certain Gregorian phrases." (F)

381. "The question of pronunciation of Latin is closely bound up with that of the restoration of Gregorian chant, the constant subject of Our thoughts and recommendations from the very beginning of Our pontificate. The accent and pronunciation of Latin has great influence on the melodic and rhythmic formation of the Gregorian phrase, and secondly it is important that these melodies should be rendered in the same manner in which they were artistically conceived at their first beginning." (E)

382. " 'If the psalm prays, pray with it; if it weeps, weep; if it sings of joy, rejoice; if it speaks of hope, hope; if it expresses fear, fear.' (St. Agustine). How is this possible, many will ask, since we do not know Latin? How is it possible, uttered in an unknown tongue? It is true that many do not understand the official language of the Church. Let those who can, at any rate, study and digest the sense of the words thoroughly. Their piety will profit thereby, and their singing gain greatly in beauty and expressiveness. As for the rest of the faithful, with a little good will they may arrive at the same results. The liturgical texts have been faithfully translated. Follow these translations and consult them. Read the English text of the Offices beforehand; you will soon become inbued with the general meaning of the words which you will have to sing." (F)

383. "In Low Masses and Offices which are not strictly liturgical, such as triduums and novenas, and during the exposition of the Blessed Sacrament, singing is allowed even in the vulgar tongue, provided that both literary text and music have been approved by competent ecclesiastical authority." (D)

VII. Rubrics

384. "It is not lawful to make the Priest at the altar wait any longer than the ceremonies allow for the sake of the singing or instrumental music." (A)

385. "It is only allowed to sing a motet in honor of the Blessed Sacrament after the *Benedictus* at High Mass. A short motet with words approved by the Church may also be added after the proper Offertory of the Mass has been sung." (A)

386. "Let it be noted that it is not permissible to omit any one of the prescribed parts, common or proper, of the Mass, Office, or any other function. All the antiphons of the psalms and canticles, must be repeated all through when the rite requires it. When, as is sometimes allowed, one portion of the liturgical text can be replaced by the organ, this text is to be recited in the choir in a voice which can be plainly heard and understood, or by the choristers themselves *recto tono*." (D)

387. "During Low Masses solemnly celebrated, motets may be sung or the organ played, in accordance with the rubric. But this must be so contrived that the chants and organ playing are only heard when the priest is not reciting prayers aloud, that is, during the preparation and thanksgiving, from the Offertory to the Preface, from the *Sanctus* to the *Pater Noster* and from the *Agnus Dei* to the Post-Communion. Voice and organ must cease during the recitation of the *Confiteor* and the *Ecce Agnus Dei* if Communion be given." (D)

388. "We have to point out that it is in error to suppose, as some have done, that in non-liturgical or extra-liturgical Offices one may perform musical compositions in free style which have already been condemned or pronounced unsuitable for the liturgical Offices. It is only fitting on the contrary to insist upon a dignified and serious style for all music rendered in God's House in the course of any sacred function whatsoever; for that of the solemn liturgy, other and special rules are laid down." (D)

389. "The hymns of the Church must keep their traditional form. It is not lawful, for instance, to compose a *Tantum Ergo* in such a way that the first verse is a romance, an aria or an adagio and the *Genitori* an allegro." (A)

390. "The *Tantum Ergo* and *Genitori* before the benediction of the Blessed Sacrament must be immediately followed by the Oremus and the Benediction, as in the actual course of these ceremonies it is not permissible to sing anything either in Latin or in the vulgar tongue." (D)

391. "The *Kyrie, Gloria, Credo*, etc. must represent the unity of their text in the music." (A)

392. "According to the laws of the Church, the *Sanctus* of the Mass must be finished before the Elevation; wherefore in this point the celebrant must attend to the singers." (A)

393. "The *Gloria* and *Credo*, according to Gregorian tradition, should be comparatively short." (A)

VIII. Organ

394. "Although the proper music of the Church is only vocal, the accompaniment of an organ is allowed." (A)

395. "There is one musical instrument, however, which properly and by tradition belongs to the Church, and that is the organ. On account of its grandeur and majesty it has always been considered worthy to mingle with liturgical rites, whether for accompanying the chant, or, when the choir is silent, for eliciting soft harmonies at times." (B)

396. "Since vocal music must always be predominant, the organ and instruments may only sustain but never crush it." (A)

397. "All organ playing must be performed not only according to the character of the instrument but also according to the rules of sacred music as described above." (A)

398. "It is unlawful to introduce the singing with long preludes or to interrupt it with impromptu interludes." (A)

399. "Let that organ music alone resound in our churches which expresses the majesty of the place and breathes the sanctity of the rites; for in this way both the art of organ builders and that of the musicians who play the organ will be revived and render good service to the sacred liturgy." (B)

400. "On the Ferias and Sundays of Advent and Lent, except Gaudete and Laetare Sundays, no instrument whatever must be played, even simply as an accompaniment to the voices. Yet a discreet accompaniment is allowed if solely to sustain the voices, and this only when Gregorian chant is sung and in case of real necessity, acknowledged by us. The use of any instrument whatsoever even merely as an accompaniment to the voices remains absolutely forbidden in the Offices of the last three days of Holy Week." (D)

401. "In some Masses of Requiem the organ or harmonium is allowed, but only to accompany the voices. At Low Masses of Requiem no instrument whatever must be played."

IX. Other Instruments

1. General.

402. "In any special case, within the proper limits and with due care, other instruments may be allowed but never without special permission of the Bishop of the diocese." (B)

403. "As we have learned that attempts are being made in different places to revive a kind of music which in no way befits the sacred Offices, particularly on account of its immoderate use of instruments, We hereby declare that chant combined with orchestra is by no means considered by the Church as a more nearly perfect form of music or more suited to sacred things. It is proper that the voice itself rather than musical instruments should be heard in the churches; that is, the voice of the clergy, singers and congregation. It must not be thought that the Church is opposed to the advance of musical art in preferring the human voice to any instrument, but no instrument, however excellent and perfect, can surpass the human voice in expressing the feelings of the soul, most of all when it is used by the mind to offer prayer and praise to Almighty God." (B)

2. Piano.

404. "The use of the piano is forbidden in churches as also that of all noisy or irreverent instruments such as drums, kettledrums, cymbals, triangles, etc." (A)

3. Bands.

405. "Bands are strictly forbidden to play in Church and only for some special reason after the consent of the Bishop has been obtained may a certain number of specially chosen wind instruments be allowed; and the music they play must always be reverent and appropriate and in every way like the organ." (A)

406. "Bands may be allowed by the Bishop in processions outside the church as long as they do not perform secular music." (A)

407. "Without special permission, to be applied for on each separate occasion from the Apostolic Visita, no instrument except the organ or harmonium is to be played in the Church and notice is hereby given that it is not our intention to grant such permission except in altogether exceptional and peculiar circumstances. Authorization must also be sought each time that musical choirs wish to take part in outdoor processions and musical items must be confined to religious pieces, expressly composed for the purpose, or better still to accompanying a hymn sung either in Latin or in the vulgar tongue by choristers or the faithful." (D)

GENERAL INDEX
(All references are to paragraphs.)

a, pronunciation of, 235
Accelerando, 94
Accent
  nature in word, 96
  primary or tonic, 96
  secondary, 98, 108
  and ictus, 105, 109
  on rise note, 106
  on fall note, 107
  secondary melodic, 128
  brevity of, 143
  in modern music, 165
  in cadences, 203
  in chant, 381
  grammatical signs, 27
  and dynamics, 121
  in Romance languages, 96
  acute, 96
  grave, 96
Accented beat, 163
Accented syllable, 94-95
  in fall group, 133
Accidentals, 8
Adrian, Pope, 308
ae, pronunciation of, 242
Agnus Dei, 293
agogics, 121, 126, 149, 152
Alleluia, 303
  how sung, 270
  in Easter Vespers, 215
  in ordinary Vespers, 190
  at Mass, 282
Amen
  meaning of, 277, 290
  how sung, 270
Anthems, 229
Antiphon, 304
  at Introit, 278
  in Vespers, 191-192, 194, 196
Arsis (*see* Rise Group)
Asterisk
  directions for singer, 17
  in Vespers, 191, 200, 206, 219
au, pronunciation of, 242
Authentic modes (*see* Modes)
b, classification of, 253
Bands in church, 405-407
Banquet of Mass, 275, 292 ff.
Bar line
  as divisions of the melody, 12
  and breathing, 12
  in modern music, 163
Basic pulsation, 47

Benedicamus Domino
  at Mass, 295
  at Vespers, 225
Benedictus following *Sanctus*, 288-289
Benedictine Monks of Solesmes
  restoration of the chant, 318 ff.
  and chironomy, 159
Bishops, duties of, 349, 363
Bivirga, 29, 32
  as climax, 134
c, pronunciation of, 255
Cadence
  nature of, 49
  spondees in, 207
  special dactylic, 212
  in Vespers, 198, 202, 207-212
  final, 198
Capella musicorum, 342
Capitulum, 217
cc, pronunciation of, 262
ch, pronunciation of, 262
Chant
  and the Mass, 271 ff.
  restoration of, 318 ff.
  dignity of, 336 ff.
  as art, 325
  regulations for, 324 ff
  place in liturgy, 330
  reform of, 324 ff.
  qualities of, 334-335
  lectures in, 351
  time for, 354
  conducting, 153 ff.
Chapter, in Vespers, 217
Charlemagne, 308
Chironomy, 153 ff.
Choirmaster, duties of, 345, 364
Clef signs
  in general, 5
  do and *fa*, 6
  position of, 7
  history of, 310
Clerics, duties of, 345
climacus, 37
Climax
  rhythmic, 32
  in melody, 56
  in groups, 119-120
  in divisions, 124, 128, 149, 151-152
  in syllabic chants, 134(a)
  in psalms, 206
clivis, 29, 31
Comma, 13

Commemorations, in Vespers, 223
Communio (Communion hymn), 294
Commission for Church Music, 349
Consonants
  in Latin language, 232
  number of, 249
  classification of, 250
  production of, 254
  explosive, 251
  sustainable, 251
  voiced, 252
  unvoiced, 252
Credo
  place in the Mass, 285
  and text, 391
  length of, 393
Crescendo, 94
Custos (*see* Guide)
d, classification of, 253
Dactyl
  definition, 97
  and natural rhythm, 103
  and accent, 104
  and rise to accent, 129
Dactylic cadence (*see* Cadence), 103
Decrescendo, 94
Diphthongs, 240-241
Directing the chant (*see* Chironomy), 153 ff.
Dismissal in Mass, 275, 295
Division of melodies, 12-14
  nature of, 124
  how rendered, 152
do clef, 6
do line, 310
Dominant of Modes (*see* Modes), 174, 176, 182
  modern and ancient, 179, 311
  in psalms, 197
  in modern music, 172
Dominus vobiscum, 276, 284, 287
Dotted note, 49
Double phrase mark (also *see* Bar line), 12(a)
Duration
  of notes, 44
  in rhythm, 57, 60
  importance of, 60-61, 93
  of syllables, 94
  of pause in psalmody, 206
Dynamics
  definition, 121
  and rhythm, 126
  and expression, 149
e, pronunciation of, 238
ei, pronunciation of, 244
episema
  appearance in print, 15
  function, 50, 145
Epistle, 281
eu, pronunciation of, 243
E u o u a e, meaning of, 216
excelsis, pronunciation of, 268

Expression and dynamics, 149
f, classification of, 250
fa clef, 6
fa line, 310
Fall, in rhythm, 57
Fall note (or ictus)
  qualities of, 62-63, 68
  and repose, 68
  kinds of, 74
  in division, 123, 144
  in melody, 57-58
  in stress, 57, 59, 164
  in duration, 57, 60, 167
  in elementary rhythm, 65
  in simple rhythm, 75
  in time groups, 75, 79-80, 82
  in groups, 85, 86
  on accented syllable, 102, 107
  on last syllable, 99, 103-104
  in neumes, 147
  as ictus in length, 148
  in modern music, 162 ff.
Fall group (or thesis)
  nature of, 116-117
  qualities of, 118
  place for, 119
  in division, 123, 139, 145, 150
  how delineated, 154, 156
Fall divisions
  in subordinate divisions, 124
  in syllabic chants, 134
Final cadence (*see* Cadence), 198
Final in modes (*see* Modes), 174, 176
  in psalmody, 198
Flat (*see te*)
flex, in psalms, 195, 214
Foreign words, 269
Full bar (*see* Bar line)
g, classification of, 240, 256
Glide-off vowels, 240
Glide-on vowels, 240
Gloria, 279
  place in the Mass, 279
  and text, 391
  length of, 393
Gloria Patri
  in the Introit, 278
  in Vespers, 189-190, 193
gn, pronunciation of, 264
Gospel, 281, 284
Gradual, 282-283
Grave accent, 96
Greek words, pronunciation of, 269
Gregorian Chant (*see* Chant)
Gregorian Mass, 296
Gregory the Great, 307, 321
Group of notes
  definition of, 75
  nature of notes in, 79 ff.
  nature of, 116 ff.
  retain characteristics, 123
  in syllabic chants, 134(b)
  in modern music, 169

Grouping of notes
  in neumatic chants, 84-85
  in syllabic chants, 91 ff., 115
  examples of, 126-127, 129-130, 148
Guide note, 11(f)
Guido d'Arezzo, 310
Gueranger, 319-320
h, classification of, 257
Half bar (*see* Bar line)
Half tone, 3
Hebrew words, pronunciation of, 269
Hucbald, 312
Hymn
  in general, 389
  in Vespers, 218
  symmetrical division in, 14
  Ut queant laxis, 310
i, pronunciation of, 239
  before *u*, 248
ij, iij in *Kyrie*, 18
Ictus (*see* also Fall note)
  definition, 72
  other terms, 73
  place of, 85
  cannot succeed each other, 85
  in word, 99, 104
  in syllabic chants, 99, 110
  on weak syllables, 155
  independent of accent, 105
  on accent syllables, 103, 107
  on final syllables, 99, 106, 164
  on unaccented syllables, 155
  in modern music, 162
Incise
  as sign of division, 12(d)
  unequal length of, 14
  beginning with isolated note, 89
  nature of, 12(d), 127, 130
  in practice, 125 ff.
Instruments in church, 402-403
Intonation
  in Vespers, 196
  of *Magnificat*, 220
Introit, 278
Isolated note
  how treated, 87
  at beginning of melody of phrase, 88, 138
Ite missa est, 295
j, pronunciation of, 245, 258
John XIX, Pope, 310
Joining of divisions, 137 ff.
Jubilus, 282
Keys for Gregorian melodies
  in relation to modern scale, 4
  choice of key, 185-186
  for psalms, 231
Kyrie, 278, 391
l, classification of, 253
Latin pronunciation
  vowels, 234 ff.
  consonants, 249 ff.
  diphthongs, 240 ff.

and foreign words, 269
  use of, 380-381
Leading tone, 179
Leaps in chant, 147
Length of Gregorian note, 46
  signs of, 48 ff.
Leger lines, 7
Legislation of church music, 322 ff.
Lessons at Mass, 281
Liber Usualis, 189
Life through rhythm, 77
Liquescent notes
  appearance, 11(e)
  purpose of, 43
Liturgy
  definition of, 271
  nature of, 324-325, 330
Low Masses, 383, 387
m, classification of, 253
Magnificat, 220
Mass, liturgical division of, 275 ff.
Measure in modern music, 82
Mediant cadence, 198
Melismatic chants, 19(c)
Melodic climax, 119, 124, 130
Melody
  divisions of, 12, 14
  kinds of, 19
  in chant, 20-21
  natural melody of word, 111-112, 130
Member, 12(c), 89
  nature of, 128, 131
Men in choir, 371-372
Mocquereau, 321
Modes
  in general, 172 ff.
  formula of, 173
  division of, 175-176
  transposed, 178
  study of, 182
  characteristics of, 180-181
  melodies of, 184
Monosyllabic words, 204
Mora vocis, 127
Motets, 387
Music
  sacred, 325, 327 ff., 33
  classical, 341
  modern, 343
n, classification of, 253
Natural sign, 10
Neumatic chants, 19(b)
Neumes
  in general, 24-27
  kinds of, 28-29
  of two notes, 29
  of three notes, 33
  compound, 42
  special, 43
  in selection, 143
Non-Latin words, pronunciation of, 269
Non-liturgical services, 388

Notes
  shape of, 1, 11, 62
  nature of, 123
  on staff, 2
  square, 11(a)
  inclined, 11(b)
  virga, 11(c)
  quilisma, 11(d)
  liquescent, 11(e)
  guide, 11(f)
  dotted, 49
  isolated, 87-88
  in modern music, 166
Notker, Blessed, 309
Novenas, 383
o, pronunciation of, 236
oe, pronunciation of, 242
Offertory, 275, 286
Orchestra in church, 403
Ordinaries, duties of, 345, 363
Oremus, 280, 286
oriscus, 41
Organ
  use of, 394 ff.
  in Requiem Masses, 401
  at other services, 400
Organist, duties of, 366
p, classification of, 253
Participation of the faithful, 272, 313, 367-369
Palestrina, 341
Pastors, duties of, 358, 360-361
Pauses (*see* Duration, Mora vocis, Bar line)
Peace in chant, 151
Petrus, 308
ph, pronunciation of, 257
Phrase
  division sign, 12(b)
  and isolated note, 88
  nature of, 132
  completeness of, 141
  in modern music 168, 170
Piano in church, 404
Pitch
  of Gregorian notes, 4
  and rhythm, 57-58, 93
  choice of, 185 ff.
Plagal modes (*see* Modes), 175-176
Plain chant (*see* Chant)
Plain song (*see*. Chant)
podatus, 29-30
Polyphonic music, 312, 342, 373
porrectus, 39
Pothier, 321
Preface at Mass, 287
Preparatory syllables, 203
pressus
  as sign of length, 52, 86
  in grouping, 130, 147
Priest at Mass, 274
Pronunciation of Latin, 232 ff., 381
Psalmody, 188 ff.

Psalms, structure of, 195
Pulsation, basic, 47
punctum (*see* Notes)
qu, pronunciation of, 259
Quarter bar (see Bar line)
quilisma
  shape, 11(d)
  characteristic of, 35
  rhythm of, 53
r, pronunciation of, 260
rallentando, 94
Range of modes, 174
Reciting tone of psalms, 196-197
Rectors of seminaries, duties of, 350, 352
Renaissance, 312 ff.
Relation of melody, text and rhythm, 20, 45
Religious communities, 375
Repetition, as sign of length, 51
Rhythm
  in chant, 20, 23
  nature of, 55 ff.
  elementary, 65
  simple, 75, 126
  purpose of, 76 ff.
  and text, 100
  natural rhythm of word, 100, 113, 129, 130
  in modern music, 161 ff., 171
Rise
  in rhythm, 57
  expresses activity, 67
  rendition of, 72
Rise note
  nature of, 57 ff., 64 ff.
  qualities of, 62-63, 67
  rendition of, 72
  in pitch, 58
  in duration, 60
  in division, 123
  brevity of, 143-144, 146, 167
  direction of, 155-156
  in elementary rhythm, 65-66
  in simple rhythm, 75
  in time groups, 75, 79, 80, 82
  as isolated note, 87-88
  on accented syllable, 102, 104
  in neumes, 147
  in modern music, 162 ff., 167
Rise group (or Arsis)
  essential elements, 116-117
  nature of, 118
  place for, 119
  in division, 123, 139-140, 145, 150
  how delineated, 154
Rise divisions
  in neumatic chant, 124
  in syllabic chant, 134
Romanus, 308
Rubrics, 384 ff.
s, classification of, 253
St. Gall, 308-309

Sacred music
  character, 330
  function, 325
  need for reform, 327
  qualities, 334-335
  decrees, 322 ff.
salicus
  character of, 36
  prolongation of, 53, 86
  for the leap, 146
Sanctus at Mass, 287 ff.
sc, pronunciation of, 265
Scale
  modern, 172
  Gregorian (see Modes)
  sol-fa, 3
  numbers, 2
scandicus, 34
sch, pronunciation of, 266
Schola cantorum, 362, 365
Schola puerorum, 373
School of the Mass, 275, 278
Sequence, 309
Sharps in chant, 8
Signs of division (*see* Bar line)
Singers in church, 345, 371
Solesmes, monastery of, 308-309
Sol-fa notes, 2
  pitch of, 4
  scale, 3
  names, 310
Solos in church, 376-377
Spirituality in chant, 150
Spondee, 97, 102, 104
Staff, 1
Stress
  a feature of rhythmic movement, 57
  quality of, 59
  in words, 93, 107
Suffrage in Vespers, 223
Syllabic chants, 19(a)
  grouping of, 134
Syncopation, 61
t, classification of, 250
Tantum ergo, 390
te, 8
  influence of, 9
  indicated by, 10
  in modes, 173, 179
Tempo (*see* also Agogics), 152
Text in chant
  an essential element, 20
  reading, 22
  Latin, 378
  translation of, 382
  correct pronunciation of, 380
  recitation of, 386
th, pronunciation of, 257
Thanksgiving Service at Mass, 275, 287
Thesis (*see* Fall group)
ti (*see te*)
  as dominant, 311
-ti-, pronunciation of, 267
Time groups (*see* Groups)
Tonality, 172
Tonic in modern music, 172
Tonus Peregrinus, 213
torculus, 38
Triduum, 383
tristropha, 40
Tropes, 309
Tuotila, 309
u, pronunciation of, 237
Unaccented beat in modern music, 163
Undulation, 133-134, 155
Uniting notes
  in neumatic chants, 79 ff.
  in syllabic chants, 91 ff.
  groups, 115 ff.
  divisions, 137
Unity through rhythm, 77
Unvoiced consonants, 252
v, classification of, 253
Vatican Edition, 321
Verses in psalmody, 206
Versicles, 189, 218-219, 223, 229
Vespers
  outline of, 189
  for Eastertide, 215
  for Advent, 216
Vocal exercises, 185 (footnote)
Vocal music, 394, 396, 403
Voiced consonants, 252
Vowels
  nature of, 232
  number in Latin, 233
  formation of, 234
  purity of, 248
  glide-on, 240
  glide-off, 240
Women in choir, 374-375
x, pronunciation of, 268
y, pronunciation of, 246
z, pronunciation of, 261

75759